A Gesture of Belonging

Letters from Bessie Head, 1965-1979

Bessie and Howard Head, 1968 [*T.Finley*]

A Gesture of Belonging

Letters from Bessie Head, 1965-1979

As she fell asleep, she placed one soft hand over
her land. It was a gesture of belonging.
[*A Question of Power* (1973): closing lines]

edited by
Randolph Vigne

SA Writers,
London

Heinemann
Portsmouth NH

SA Writers
25a Greencroft Gardens, London NW6 3LN

Heinemann Educational Books, Inc.
261 Hanover Street
Portsmouth, NH 03801

First published 1991 in Great Britain by SA Writers
and in the United States of America by Heinemann Educational
Books, Inc.

*A CIP catalogue record for this book
is available from the British Library.*

ISBN 1-872086-04-7 (SA Writers)
ISBN 0-435-08059-8 (Heinemann)

Set in 10/14 Trump Medieval by Robert Vicat Ltd., London
Printed and bound in Great Britain by
Cox and Wyman, Reading, Berkshire

CONTENTS

Preface

The Bessie Head archive in Serowe contains several thousand letters she sent and received. Nearly all of them date from 1970, the year after her first novel, *When Rain Clouds Gather*, was published. That event started a voluminous correspondence with publishers, agents and readers. Her earlier letters are in the hands of the correspondents to whom she wrote them. Of the 107 surviving letters I received from her between 1965 and 1979, 33 were written in the first five years of her life in exile, the period almost unrepresented in the archive.

She was a superb correspondent, dealing with letters promptly, actually answering what was said in those she received, and writing always vividly and with passion. It is highly desirable that a definitive edition of her letters should one day appear, perhaps when the people she wrote about, and those she fell out with, can no longer suffer from what she said about them. Those she wrote me are of special interest because they describe her life in Botswana before she became known and contain much that influenced the writing of her books. They also, perhaps, show her capacity for a close personal relationship, which is referred to in the title I have chosen for this collection, giving her words at the end of *A Question of Power* an extended meaning of which I hope she would approve.

She reproached me for using, without asking her, a letter of hers in *The New African* magazine (VII, 1, 1968), which I then edited. She heaped coals of fire by sending with her reproaches a marvellous article, "Africa and Revolutions", for the magazine. I cannot ask her permission now but feel she would agree that her letters, being part of her writings which so many love and admire, should be shared. Hurtful or libellous passages have been cut, as she would have wished.

Their publication may give people who did not know Bessie an opportunity to learn what she was like, especially in the hard early years of her exile. I hope the letters will show them that, with her death on 17 April 1986, the light that went out was a bright and inspiring one, however dark the scenes of her life that it illuminated.

I am most grateful to Ruth Forchhammer, librarian of the Khama III Memorial Museum, Serowe, for sending me copies of seven letters Bessie wrote me which I had lost and of all of those extant that I wrote her from 1969 onwards. And even more for the care that she and her sponsors, with Danish funding, are taking of Bessie Head's papers in Serowe. This book is for them, for Patrick van Rensburg and for Howard Head.

Introduction

My first awareness of Bessie Head was of a young woman journalist who had come to Cape Town from Johannesburg in, I think, 1961 and was working for *Golden City Post*, a weekly tabloid newspaper with a black readership. Though *Post* took pains not to offend the authoritarian apartheid government on major issues, it went in for hectically worded crusades on minor matters of race discrimination. The newcomer — whom I heard about from Ken Mackenzie, Cape Town manager of *Post's* stable-mate, the pioneering illustrated monthly, *Drum* — was said to be a fire-eating African nationalist and a supporter of the Pan-Africanist Congress (PAC).

Led by her hero, Robert Mangaliso Sobukwe, whom I too held in deep respect, the PAC had been banned during the State of Emergency following the national campaign it had mounted in 1960. Its Positive Action Campaign is now best remembered for the police firing on an unarmed crowd at the obscure Johannesburg township of Sharpeville. The leadership, Sobukwe at the head, had led its following into the country's prisons, where many were held for years to come. The campaign had had its greatest success in Cape Town, where the entire African community went on strike; 40,000 African men marched almost on parliament itself to demand both negotiations with the repressive government led by Dr Verwoerd and the release of their leaders. The resulting political atmosphere of the early 1960s was electric, for those committed to radical change in South Africa. It was made even more highly charged by the iron-fisted, repressive actions of the Afrikaner Nationalist government and its Security Police. Such an atmosphere could be both a challenge and a threat to the emotionally finely-tuned and the psychologically unstable.

Bessie Emery (the surname was that of her mother's Aus-

1

tralian husband), then about 24 or 25, had come originally from Natal — she told me many years later about her white mother and African father, orphanage life and fostering — and had trained as a teacher. Her great love was writing, however, and her work at *Post* was interspersed with producing sketches and short stories, upon which Ken Mackenzie would helpfully comment.

She soon became part of our large circle of political activists and writers, and married another recent arrival from the Transvaal, Harold Head, with whom I had become friendly quite separately. She wrote in 1963, in an early contribution to *Transition*, the literary monthly from Uganda, that in South Africa "one always and only meets one's friends through politics", and at that time the comradeship among the activist opponents of racial supremacy in South Africa was strong and widespread.

The Heads made a home in a rooming house in District Six, the old "Coloured" ghetto near the heart of Cape Town, later totally obliterated by bulldozers in the cause of racial segregation. I remember the Heads' rooms quite well — the vivid magazine cut-outs pinned to the walls, the sparse furniture, and books and papers everywhere.

Bessie was a bright and talkative person, but many found her alarming and feared both her deadly, silent stare of disapproval, and her furious outbursts when her fiercely held Africanist views were offended. Harold and she also quarrelled a lot, and she would rage at him in the presence of others.

In January 1962 some friends and I combined to launch a new monthly journal. The name *The New African* signalled the journal's identification with the new Africa of decolonisation and high ideals, of which we saw South Africa as part. We scorned the frontier between politics and culture, between South Africa and the rest of the continent, and, all of us being members of the militant wing of the non-racial South African Liberal Party, between racial groups. Bessie sent us her only published poem, "Things I don't like," for our July 1962 issue and we published six of her stories and articles between then and 1964.

One of her more famous outbursts was prompted by the

advice of a white Communist woman acquaintance that she should "help her own people" instead of writing for *The New African*. We ran the magazine on less than a shoestring and were in frequent trouble with the Security Police, who, among other harassments, confiscated two entire issues and later had us charged under the Obscene Publications Act.

Harold Head scraped a living in freelance journalism and, a competent administrator, also earned a small sum running the circulation of *The New African* and helping with the Liberal fortnightly news magazine *Contact*. Under Patrick Duncan's editorship *Contact* had grown in stature since its total defiance of Emergency restrictions on reporting in 1960. In 1963 the Heads, with their small baby Howard, moved to Port Elizabeth, where Harold became the first black reporter on *Evening Post*, the only progressive daily in the country at that time.

We were a small, embattled group, with friends in the equally embattled Congress Alliance, whose Cold War affiliation we did not share, among African nationalists, and democratic socialists. We had links too with a growing number of political exiles in Europe and America. The post-Emergency suppression of political action and protest across the colour line reduced our activities and forced some of us instead into underground, armed resistance. The African National Congress set up Umkhonto we Sizwe, the PAC tried to harness an African jacquerie called Poqo, and a collection of Liberals, socialists and African nationalists came together in the National Committee for Liberation (later to become known as the African Resistance Movement, ARM). All three came to grief in 1963-4 and ours, the ARM, was completely shattered after the chance arrest of a key member in a police raid on 4 July 1964. Many of us were arrested and some, of whom I was one, got away.

I arrived in England in August 1964 and my wife and children soon joined me. Most of us had scattered. Harold arrived in London not long afterwards, escaping constant harassment from the Security Police. His and Bessie's quarrels had got the better of them and she had taken the baby, Howard, with her to the British Protectorate of Bechuanaland (now the Republic of Botswana). She had been allowed to leave South Africa, a few months before my escape, on a one-way exit permit. This was to enable her to take up a teaching post at the Tshekedi Memorial School in the northern village of Serowe, capital of the Bamangwato community, who had played such a major role in their country's history. A friend from Liberal Party days, Patrick van Rensburg, had already settled near Serowe with his British wife, to start a school called Swaneng Hill.

This was the end of the comradeship we had shared. It had begun to disintegrate well before this — her 1963 *Transition* article was a valediction to those who had already left. "Now they are all gone, those brave, optimistic characters! One misses them furiously!" Bessie had written, and the life of a newcomer to remote Botswana was in painful contrast to the eve-of-Waterloo atmosphere of our lives in the South African cities, and in Cape Town most of all, in the early 1960s.

The New African resumed publication in London in March 1965, again under my editorship and Neville Rubin's management. I heard nothing from Bessie, however, until the arrival of a letter in November 1965 [1], which coincided with a visit from Robin Farquharson, like me a friend of both Harold's and Bessie's. Robin was a very sick man and could do much less for Bessie than he would have wished, heavily drugged as he was in the course of the severe mental illness which was to lead to his death only a few years later. Robin, one of the most brilliant of his generation in South Africa, was soon to lose his fellowship at Churchill College, Cambridge and to be cast adrift. Was he a victim of the pressures of the South Africa that had forced out so many of us after our failed challenges to the Afrikaner Nationalist regime? Was M, another close friend of the Heads, who became schizophrenic in exile in London, another such victim [28, 53]? Was Bessie herself? One should rather ask whether any physical factor, perhaps genetic, would alone have brought them to madness or something like it.

From the early months of her first stay in Serowe there were signs of a coming breakdown. She wrote in one of the first short stories she sent me from there:

It's just that I have a desperate need to communicate and it

4

The New African

No. 52 AFRICA 3/- U.S.A./CANADA 70c U.K. 4/- OTHERS 5/-

DADIÉ

DIPOKO

NKOANA

OKAI

NYERERE

AIDOO BULANE HUDDLESTON BESSIE HEAD

A Salahi illustration from Salih's 'Wedding of Zein'

ARMAH CESAIRE SITHOLE NGUGI

Cover of the 52nd issue of *The New African*

5

may be that a stranger somewhere would comprehend my suffering and help me. That is why I am putting down everything. Even if I am insane, at least someone could help me to accept and I should have peace of mind. ("For 'Napoleon Bonaparte', Jenny and Kate", *Southern African Review of Books*, August/ October 1990)

Yet Bessie's own case seemed to fit none of the usual labels. She was neither paranoid nor schizophrenic, manic-depressive nor psychotic. In the simplest terms, she was in no proper sense "mad". The product of a deeply disturbing, insecure childhood, tortured by her status as a "Coloured" (while belonging to no community designated by that term in the evil system of apartheid), constantly brooding on the story of her mother's mental illness and her own conception, she was haunted by an abiding sense of alienation and aloneness, the fear of madness and the sense of a coming early death. Yet, at 26 or 27, when I last saw her in Cape Town, despite being the "great pan-Africanist on a soap-box" she later called herself [3] and the household shrew who suffered Harold's failings not at all, she had a gaiety and sweetness, a childlike gravity, which did not fully conceal her seriousness of purpose. Nor her sense of destiny as a writer. She cast no shadow of the "madness" that was later to haunt her.

In response to her early letters from Serowe, Robin, sick as he was, and I found some money for her and threw out such a lifeline as we could, barely keeping Bessie afloat in the stormy seas she was so temperamentally ill-equipped to navigate. Her friends were concerned with her physical survival and that of her small child, with her status as a refugee, once she had parted company with the Tshekedi Memorial School, with plans to find her grants or bursaries to study or work in other countries, and with the struggle to create conditions in which she could write the books which were so devoutly believed in by a few of us at that early stage. Among those few were Robin Farquharson, Kenneth Mackenzie (by then in London), Myrna Blumberg (married to Ken and also earlier in the heart of our Cape Town set), Vreni Oleram (a young International Voluntary Service worker returned from Serowe where she had typed Bessie's manuscripts), Rose-

6

Innes Phahle (a South African teacher in London who had met Bessie in Botswana), Oliver Caldecott (publisher and *New African* cartoonist), James Currey (ex-Oxford University Press, Cape Town, who brought Bessie to Heinemann) and, in South Africa, Patrick Cullinan, (Transvaal farmer and poet), the political campaigner and poet Dennis Brutus, then on Robben Island — and the indispensable anchor in Serowe, Pat van Rensburg.

The letters that follow fall into sequences written from her various addresses. They call for little elucidation or comment from me: such as seems necessary will appear after each sequence. I have not attempted to draw from the letters any lessons about literature or life, but Bessie Head was a remarkably gifted writer caught in a painful dilemma from which there was to be no escape. Her books are the carefully worked product of the gift and the dilemma and much in the letters is their product too, but before recollection in tranquillity. Perhaps the letters are at times the equal of the stories. "Something that is created out of intense despair has a swing and flow of its own," she wrote. "You make a complete statement." They are often the transmutation of despair into optimism [6].

She wrote also before the publication of her first novel, *When Rain Clouds Gather*: "I could get a lot of things written down just now, partly from desperation and partly to drain out all the things I love here". It must be said that there is more of the desperation in the letters than of the things she loved in her Botswana exile. In "For Serowe: a Village in Africa", written for *The New African* just at this time, in "Looking for a Rain-god" (*The New African*, April 1966) and in "Chibuku Beer and Independence" (*The New African*, November 1966) is the Botswana seldom found in the letters. She ended her worm's-eye-view of the Botswana independence celebrations, in Francistown, when she was near her lowest ebb:

"It is all right," I thought. "The whole world seems topsy-turvy but there is something here in this country that is good. Perhaps it is a weird kind of people who pull against the current; unprovokable; ever reasonable. Perhaps it is the rags and tatters of poverty that are worn with an upright posture and pathetic dignity. Whatever it is I say it is good because you feel it in your heart as peace."

The hard words she had for her Batswana hosts at that time she rationalised years later in an essay in *World Literature Written in English*, vol 18, 1 (1979). Coming from South Africa, from "an oppressed people [who] do not know what it is like to have our ambitions aroused [or to] see liberation on an immediate horizon," in Botswana "I found the people, initially, extremely brutal and harsh, only in the sense that I had never encountered human ambition and greed before in a black form".

To a friend who figures in the letters and who asked me "But are they interesting?" when I told her they were to be published, I could only answer flatly: "Yes, to those who found Bessie so and enjoyed her books". Perhaps they have a wider interest. She was a remarkable person both as a writer, and as a student of what we called "L.life". A Johannesburg academic correspondent of hers wrote, revealingly, "whenever I saw a Botswanan stamp in the post I would mentally groan," (Susan Gardner, *Hecate*, 12, 1-2, 1986). Despite the difficulties they created for a fellow exile like me, and for all the anguish in some of them, that Botswana stamp had a very different effect on me. I only hope I told you so, Bessie, and that the sentence was legible.

1. Serowe (1)
27 October 1965 – September 1966

[1]

P.O. Box 130, Serowe
27 October 1965

Dear Randolph,

I don't know if you might remember me — BESSIE Head. It is a long while since I wrote to you.

I am just writing to you because there's a dim chance that I'll be alive or see this year to an end here. Such tremendous pressure has built up against me in this little village and I shall get no help from the police if my life is in danger.

I was just living here like the greatest hermit you can find. Days and days of silence. I can get by like that and I needed it.

Little by little I became aware of the most terrible brutality in this quiet-seeming village. Nothing ever happens. There are only people and animals here and starvation, fear, frustration and dog-eat-dog.

Nobody values anybody except for what he/she can give so everything's rather that crazy thing — survival of the fittest.

The authorities have made no bones about the fact that they don't want me here. I have been trying in every way to get out. They're all engaged from the Republic of S. Africa. They've never stopped at showing me what they think of me.

Apart from that I'm not exactly loved by the Batswanas here. I shouldn't really care — there's only a kind of rat-race, royalty, society you can revolve in anyway.

The women kind of treat men like property. Same with the men. Then there's all this feverish hopping about looking for "SOMETHING." It's a fever and hell here — everybody's sex organs. Apart from I-can-stick-around-alone-attitude; I also like to keep my sex organs to myself.

Well; the women don't love me. They think I'm playing a new game to their disadvantage. The men are vicious brutes when they can't get a woman to bed.

There is a man here, the principal of our school — he sort of thought he could get started to sleep with me — just like a frenzied itch but as a woman I mean nothing — when he couldn't get rid of the itch he just turned on me — right to the point of manhandling me in front of the kids and twisting my arm. I had to bite his hand to let him let go. This happened Monday 25/10/65. I fled away from the school, screaming. He went and called the police — that I had gone out of my mind. They came to my home and took me to the charge office.

This isn't the first occasion. I enclose a letter as proof that this is true. It's from the secretary who is in charge of schools. They had an emergency meeting and forced me to return. I told them my sanity can't stand it.

I am at such a low ebb, Randolph. I have always just been myself and there's nothing so wonderful in that. Now that I feel my life so threatened I do want to stay alive and I shan't if I don't get out of here.

If I really crack mentally I'm done for. I have my son here with me.

Could something be done. The police sort of told me that for biting the fellow I couldn't expect them to approve of my residence here. No question that I was defending myself. See.

You know Pat Cullinan. He has helped me tremendously. I did some writing here and he's trying to get it published for me. I can't ask for more help from him. He's doing so much.

10

I've also completely broken with Harold. It's just like that.

You know John Shingler? He's now in America. He was with Nusas. He referred my name to the Canadian Union of Students for a scholarship. They wrote asking me to apply. But this takes time — to hear from them.

I also heard about Amnesty. Could they help me? Could you get at them there in London? Even if they could let me out of here — out of Africa which is a peculiar hell just now. UNO, UNESCO wants people to help. It's my only hope if I can get at them one day.

I am interested in botany with a view to doing plant research. I thought this could be useful knowledge for food production and if I were of use to a government my life wouldn't be at the mercy of every cheap Tom, Dick, Harry with a sex itch. It's pretty terrible I tell you for a woman to be alone in Africa. Men treat women as the cheapest commodity.

I don't feel coherent. I hope you can read between the lines as to how urgent my predicament is.

Also I've hardly survived on this salary of £16. R32. Debts have piled and piled. If I had to get the scholarship I couldn't leave with the debts.

Food bill	R 55
Clothes	25
Advances	24
	R104 or £52

(Everything is sky high price. Haven't been able to eat porridge and meat which is the teacher's diet.)

Also have nothing practically as far as clothes go. This R25 clothes bill was from last year for skirt and blouses. That's all. Do you think I could get any assistance from Amnesty. Do they have scholarships.

Yours sincerely, Bessie Head

[2]

P.O. Box 130, Serowe
11 November 1965

Dear Randolph,

The School Committee asked me to undergo medical examination to test my sanity. I refused. It's humanely impossible. I am without a job now. Never got anywhere with Pat van Rensburg. Very reserved, abstract man.

Randolph, they've pushed things for me. There's not anyone cares to talk to me. Even normal person can get shaken to say: "Let's see if you're sane or insane." God knows what I am. Expect only myself just holding on. Got no one.

Bess

[3]

Compare w/ Mani... her experience @school... margaret.

P.O. Box 130, Serowe
15 November 65

Dear Randolph,

Sent you a short note. The school committee wanted me to get myself certified sane/insane which I could not do because it is

1. Humiliating

2. If they want to destroy me — why? I want to leave Bechuanaland. Don't care a hell about their politics. Things I love in Africa are far above hatred, jealousy etc.

3. Does this insanity business now block all my chances of getting to another country? They can tell the other governments they think I'm insane. People have worked this against me here and the police too. All the refugees get hell. I

resigned immediately from teaching. Past four days have been unearthly. My son got terribly sick — retched solidly. He's all right now. Did not get in touch with Pat van Rensburg but with friends I spent Christmas with, Mary and Martin Kibblewhite. They teach at Swaneng. They also put me in touch with David Wylde. He said his cousin made an error. He'd never dream of travelling through Africa. No rifle. Too many wild animals and revolutions!!

But I can check with the refugees in Francistown as to how they get out. Pull strings that side like hell for me Randolph, please. I intend to stay alive. There are useful things to do on this earth and I don't intend busting up anybody's show. Just surprised people want so desperately to bust me up. Got to find a level of survival. Got to get some cranky feelings out of my system. Actually, B. Head, great pan-Africanist on a soap-box, has made a hell of a climb-down. Always said people were people but never practised what I preached. All this Africa my Africa — black people can be more cruel than most people because we lack so much and want so much. God knows I'll have to live somewhere in Africa but now am in need of some country to keep me alive till I can do useful work.

Don't bother to get in touch with Harold [Head]. I don't write to him anymore.

Not true that book of short stories is coming out in USA Sent Pat Cullinan about 15 pieces of work which he is trying to peddle carefully to get me established as a writer. Said it takes time. That's okay. He got things typed for me. Some he said were unpublishable in their present form. I enclose two of them. I also enclose a short handwritten piece for your consideration.

Sincerely,
Bessie

[4]

P.O. Box 130, Serowe
27 November 1965

Dear Randolph,

You sound as dismayed as Pat Cullinan when I told him about this "insanity" business. Pat Cullinan knows, from September, every single detail of how things have been piling up against me here. If I'd gone to the doctor they'd have certified me insane and deported me back to a mental asylum in S. Africa. This is a ruthlessly cruel place and the principal is just a pawn in the whole show to get rid of me. There are powerful people in the background fixing things. It's going to be God's own miracle if I get out of here alive. Don't know anyone here and have kept to myself most of the time but somehow people are in a frenzy about me. Have all my mail opened. Have the police terrorising anyone who talks to me.

You know perhaps nothing about a little village. Everything is in-woven and everything about everyone known. And *in an African village it's goddam deep and dangerous*. I was a damn fool to get stuck up in a village like this and not make enough efforts to get out when things were going haywire.

Randolph, I'm holding on here till something can be fixed — I'll explain later. If I don't get out alive there are a few things I want you to know.

Apart from the principal and his lecherous designs, one of the V.I.P.s of the "royal" family got big eyes for me too. Not much to the liking of his female. There was talk of doing me in last year, she said so, so he cooled off making eyes at me. But I have been watched day and night. And still am — now more than ever. All this must sound very funny and melodramatic but it's true. Think Pat van Rensburg knows what's

14

going on under the surface and wouldn't like to be involved. Otherwise he's a fine man. Since I've been jobless I've got a lot of moral support from people at his school. He has young people there from the International Voluntary Service and they're quite something new in this world — like the ideal that there's going to be peace on earth and no more war.

Pat van Rensburg's okay and his world is very sane and practical and well organised. Besides he's pulling ahead calmly against terrific odds and handicaps and his powers of organisation are what's keeping everything going. There are a lot of pullers-down in Southern Africa and in a crappy tribal society there are a hell of a lot — mostly half-crazy black people who don't know where they're going — half-crazy through constant fear and dog-eat-dog policy which is all they have known from the chiefs and colonial authorities.

Perhaps this letter too will be opened and read. I don't want to die here and there are certain people e.g. the female of the V.I.P., who just don't intend letting me get out of here alive. My God, Randolph, I'm a hell of an ugly woman — I don't know why I'm in so much trouble. It's never happened to me before. Not the kind of woman men take a second look at but HERE I've created chaos and confusion — even to the point of having my sanity threatened.

If only they knew — I'm just my own odd self. From life there is little that I want. So very little. I have my own odd solitary way of living and although unconventional it is also … [*rest of letter missing*]

Bess

She didn't like Africans but did...

> Maru

She felt like a Masarwa

[5]

P.O. Box 130, Serowe
23 December 1965

Dear Randolph,

I have been in an absolute panic that you did not receive my last letter. So I am writing to enquire if you did.

The mess I'm in is so dreadful that I'd just long for some sane normal routine again. Just want to get away from Southern Africa. Just sit here in a limbo day after day and don't know how its going to end

Pat van Rensburg said he'd try to do something. He gave me a UNO bursary form to fill in. They plan study programmes. Thought it best if I could get to Israel through UNO. They had to do everything from scratch and most probably have volumes on how to relieve the misery of poverty. Also a country like Kenya suffers terribly from erosion and if I had some useful knowledge I could apply for citizenship there.

I am very afraid my presence may not be tolerated here for long. I asked for only two months to arrange some alternative for myself. Apart from that this not knowing where I'm going next or what to do is excruciating. Have been so badly shaken have lost my nerve and desperately need to feel I can do something useful. Did Robin [Farquharson] get in touch with you?

Yours sincerely,
Bessie

[6]

P.O. Box 130, Serowe
24 December 65

Dear Randolph,

You've no idea how relieved I am. Howard is quite alright. See, I thought I'd been cut off so I sent letters in all directions; under-cover style. We people from down there always get like that when we have a bust-up with the authorities. It's terrible!!

Well I could hang on here if I could get busy right away. Here's the plan: —

1. If you could get some of my writing from Pat Cullinan you'd see it's not much — even the novel. Pat said the flights of fancy are not so good but some stuff where I analyse the commonplace is okay. There's one piece I'm dreadfully keen on. It's a short story about a jackal-blanket maker; entitled "Earth Love." My God, Randolph it's the best thing I ever wrote. I feel that. I hope Pat sends it to you; because I sent my copy to *African Review* and they used the "Old Woman" — being so socially conscious. Also Dennis Brutus sent two pieces of my work to Robin. Did he receive them? What I'd like is if possible these could be used to get some money for me: then

2. I'd get working on a long piece of work. I was going to do it anyway because what I know about Africa is Bechuanaland — not the goddam politicians but the inner release I felt on arrival here and also what I have gained — the necessary assurance to get to grips with whatever creative potential I have. There were so many hours of brooding loneliness; time for reflection. I went to a young lady here who is a volunteer from International Voluntary Service. She said she'd type out my book for me.

3. The "Old Woman" went over well. I've not heard an end of it — yet it's so simple. Going to be re-printed in War On Want magazine soon. Stencilled copies have been made here and it's to be distributed round Bechuanaland too. Well maybe these scholarships don't turn up — so maybe I turn up as a writer. I'm willing to have a try. Some of my writing had nasty things to say about Africa. There are ways of thought and life that have to be broken down and I have attacked what I don't like — especially the disregard and degradation of women. It's terrible.

4. Tell them they would not get a run-of-the-mill kind of book from me. I only love what is fresh and wild and new.

5. Could I relay some short stories and bits and bits of short things to you? The Volunteer young lady has begun to type them out for me. I have no typewriter.

Pat van Rensburg gave me £25 a few weeks ago. It's almost used up now. Prepared to battle it out like hell. Ha! Ha! Don't need Stellazine. Am a tough guy now. But admit was damn awful busted up a few weeks ago. Said to myself: "B. Head, this won't do. Pull thyself together." Well there's my son. He talks so and is full of fun and tricks these days. Every sentence begins: "I think I shall ..." in real old man style. He *thinks* he'll do this and that. Not at all like me and mad about engines and motor-cars. Am writing some P.S.s on back of page 1 and 2.

Bessie

P.S. 1 When life is a dreadful pain and bleak you sort of counter this with an opposite feeling. The day I wrote short story about the Jackal-blanket maker was indeed a *vile* day. Then I happened to see a postage stamp of a flamingo bird flying against a brilliant red sunset. And out of this emerged a strange and tender man coming home to his wife after

18

months hunting the jackal in the wild bush. It wrote itself because I was intensely unhappy that day. I love that story intensely. Something that is created out of intense despair has a swing and flow of its own. You make a COMPLETE statement. I could write a book like THAT — NOW.

P.S. 2. Pat C. said Nadine Gordimer was selecting one of the pieces I sent him for an anthology she is compiling on African writers. Just recently Caroline de C[respigny]. was detained for 180 days and he's helping about her affairs. See how dreadful the world is?

What is an African writer? Too bad. B. Head is just B. Head now. See how *grim* you can get? Fighting like mad for your own integrity however worthless this may be to others.

[7]

P.O. Box 130, Serowe
28 December 1965

Dear Randolph,

I had some good luck. I called round at Christmas for dinner with the Van Rensburgs and then asked if there was a typewriter to spare. Here it is — and I have been feeling so good. Been working all the time — putting down things myself instead of getting someone else so I could send these off, right away. There are two flights of fancy stuff (which so pains Pat Cullinan) and two other short stories "Batu" and "Looking For A Rain God." Am leaving here to-day, 28th, back to my hut!

I don't know if you can do anything with these for me or hand them on to someone else. I could get a lot of things written down just now partly from desperation and partly to drain out all the things I loved here because God knows

19

where I'm going next and I don't like that feeling very much. I'm old now. I must say Pat van Rensburg gave me a hell of a drubbing. He said I should not have exploded like that. Rather like an orderly world without volcanoes. I don't feel so good too — rather an awful failure.

What I don't like is hanging around doing just god-awful NOTHING. I could fix myself up with a typewriter in no time if I knew how many short stories could buy a typewriter. About how many? No use getting started on a piece of work and have to ask this and that person to do the typing. Maybe I'm paranoid and all that and an unpleasant person but I try to avoid upsetting my fellow men. I try to live as consciously alone as possible and it gets easier every day. No doubt I shall fit somewhere and perhaps things will be better someday. Just that I'm getting old now and don't like to feel a complete failure.

Yours sincerely,
Bessie

[8]

P.O. Box 130, Serowe
12 January 1966

Dear Randolph,

Of course I had to screw my eyes up for half an hour to decipher the letter. They say: Hopes soar. Anyway I have a lovely feeling inside. I once wrote to Pat Cullinan and Wendy: "In such a hostile environment I've somehow got a grip on myself. You can't really say what it is — an inner self-assurance that was lacking before. I don't know but I feel an independent kind of person. All this works well for me to think things out; to write."

Well, I got in touch with Mary and Martin Kibblewhite because, over Christmas, at Pat's place, I met the most fascinating man. He runs a farm of the tribe about 50 miles from Serowe. He just about has the answer to everything in Bechuanaland — its strange unpredictable climate — what grows and so on. The man is a friend of the Kibblewhites, so I asked Martin if I could get a job dish washing or digging weeds on the farm and so enable me to do some writing as well. At the moment I live in a hut 12ft x 12ft. I've done most of my writing with a candle on my knee at night. Those who have a spare hut won't let it to me. They're too afraid of me after I took on the authorities so. The poor lady who rented me this hut is on tenterhooks too. The police just came in and out. She has deserted her yard and fled to Mahalapye. It's just that everybody thinks I should have got it more than I did and things have not settled yet so the best I can do is to pull out of Serowe. Martin is trying to negotiate for me to go to the farm. He thought it a good idea. He has stuck by me all this while, I think, because he is a quaker by religion and they just don't believe in kicking a dog that's down.

I enclose the ghastly letter I received from the school committee. The one snag about the farm is that it is also run by the same men as the school committee. I would like to go there. I could learn a lot. Bechuanaland is entirely an agricultural country. I need that kind of background; all of its battle is against the elements and people are different — their selfishness, greed and hatreds are odd and different because of this tremendous battle to survive against overwhelming odds. I could get all I needed on this farm in concentrated form. It's an experimental venture of old, ancient methods of farming and the very new. A good book, published, may be an open sesame to more creative, constructive work.

Bess

Bamangwato African Administration,
Department of Education, P.O. Box 1, Serowe
Mrs Bessie Head, No 2690, Tshekedi Memorial School,
P.O. Box 97, Serowe

28 December 1965

Madam,

BLACKLIST!

I regret to have to inform you that the meeting of the Main School Committee held on the 16th December, 1965 decided to recommend to the Director of Education that you be blacklisted from teaching for having deserted your post.

The recommendation will be effective from 10th November, 1965.

Asst. Tribal Education Secretary

[9]

P.O. Box 130, Serowe
16 January 1966

Dear Randolph,

Your letter of 10th Jan is indeed good news. Never let it be said that B. Head can't grasp good luck as it comes. See, some of the things sent to Pat may do. He sent me a copy of everything which I partly gave away as presents or tried to get published. Therefore I have nothing of the old lot but am sending you a handwritten batch of new stuff.

Of the things sent to Pat C. and typed out by Vreni Oleram the real short stories are:

1. "The Green Tree" (already published in the East African magazine *Transition.*

2. "Summer Sun" — about drought and a lovely young lady who worked for me.

3. "Earth Love." (Can you get the title changed to "The Jackal Blanket Maker"? or will that title do.)

4. "Sorrow Food" — about a crazy politician.

5. "The Old Woman" (previously published in African Review).

Actually No 3 = "Earth Love" is the most goddam best bit of writing I ever did.

6. "The Woman from America," about a Negro woman who married a man of Africa. From her I learnt this lovely swear word — goddam!!

Then: *Cris de Coeur*. (Really crying!)

7. A long wrangling diatribe about an imaginary love affair entitled — "Where is The Hour of the Beautiful Dancing of Birds in the Sun-Wind."

"Strange Angels" is a kind of sequel to it. I sent Pat innumerable bits and bits about this imaginary love affair which pained him very much. He kept saying: "No factual meat! Out of touch with *physical* reality!!" I sent "Beautiful Dancing of Birds" to Dennis Brutus. His opinion was that it was the beginning of a gold-mine. I also sent him another sequel to it, which both, he sent to Robin F[arquharson]. That sequel must never see the light of day. It's ghastly writing but "Birds" is alright. Accept Dennis Brutus' view, when you read it, that "The Hour of the Beautiful Birds, etc" is a gold mine. Brutus is very romantic and it's the only bit of my writing he ever praised. "Strange Angels" is a good, sympathetic sequel to it. The other sequel, if it sees the light of day, will forever doom me as a writer of Africa. It virulently attacks African manhood. I was just in a bad mood that day and didn't really mean it. But I want the "Birds" if possible, published.

See, with this batch I'm sending and the six or seven you'll get from Pat C[ullinan] plus "Batu" and "Rain-God" it may be seen that they can't hold together as a collection of short stories. After all I'm such an isolated goddam outsider trying to be an African of Africa. Believe me — it's painful and just guesswork — but such desperate guesswork. Here in this batch, which has *no personal cris de coeur*, is real sweat, sweat, and blood. I guess, I grope I guess at some goddam unfathomable life I'm not really a part of. But one does not know where one belongs. I expected to get a typewriter from Pat C. but as you say you could get these typed out for me — that's okay. Here is a list of the new stuff I'm sending you: —

1. Mr Boithatelo, the Policeman.
2. De April Ball.
3. Mma-Oreeditse

Other short stories will be posted individually as soon as they are written. Not been doing much lately.

Martin Kibblewhite just called. He said the man and his wife are very agreeable to having me on the farm. They need a typist. But the matter will be brought to my deadly enemies here. All farm employees must go before the committee — same committee that blasted me! God's own miracle — if they agree in about two weeks time. Wouldn't it be better, if I got fixed up on the farm, to wait here for the scholarship? Awful difficulties could arise in England. Here I could get a goddam good saga written — a saga about the elements with dramatic, tormented monologues delivered to the elements. There'd just never be a book like it written before. And I'd be happy too. The man and his wife really want me. The place is desolate, lonely and I need hours of ruthless solitude to get written the kind of book I want to write. If the short stories can be worked into a book they'd help me but I want a novel so that I can take off as me in it — in spite of what dear Pat says I desperately want to take off on one long goddam vivid flight from physical reality. I just want a kind of ocean roar all the time.

I'm sending you what I have with me now but during the

24

week I'll get busy on some more short stories in case some of the things have to be rejected or there isn't enough material for a book.

There's all this awakening and movement towards a new destiny. I know I can catch hold of the vitality; the newness. I say so for myself — so that I may grow too.

Therefore, if Heinemann's wants to take the short stories sign me up and a book will come along too. Partly, at the bottom, is deep fright. You know, I'm the queer kind of bug that gets victimised because I'll do anything I really believe in at the moment. And I haven't got anyone on my level to communicate to. I want to establish myself on a level with people of a like mind. Otherwise I can be destroyed by the ignorant. I saw it here and I'll never forget the hell and terror of that month. I'm deeply frightened and shaken. Randolph, you've no idea how cruel a semi-literate person can be. He's really terrified of anything outside his doorstep. He has a small mind revolving in a small circle — his belly and sex organs. Anything he can't understand frightens him. They nearly killed me here and I'll never forget it. I must protect myself.

I believe there are places of fantastic beauty to describe in Africa. I'd just have a whale of a time if I can get me established as a writer of Africa.

Bess

P.S. Did not hear from John Shingler [South African student leader, who had moved to Canada]. It's possible the idea fell through. Never even heard from Douglas Ward who wrote asking me to apply for the scholarship. But things don't look so hopeless.

I do know that it is an awfully difficult business to be a writer but anyway one can try, that's all.

Yes I do remember H. Surprised. I thought he had kicked the bucket by now. He is one of the greatest alcoholics in the world but I shall never forget him for introducing me to Africa. Would have found it of course, one day, but he speeded everything up.

[10]

P.O. Box 130, Serowe
21 January 1966

Dear Randolph,

Here follows another short story. Vreni sent me an application form which I have posted to Leiden. I gave the part that needed recommendation to Pat van Rensburg.

I also met the man and his wife from the farm and they rather are wonderful people. They'll let me know if I can come. Pat got money to fix up my debts here from Canon Collins.

Don't worry if Heinemann turns the stories down.

Bess

[11]

P.O. Box 130, Serowe
27 January 1966

Dear Randolph,

Let me know whether you received these two stories:

1. Laughing at the Birds.
2. Those who flee.

They'll be posted at a date later because I am still awaiting a little money. I shall keep writing others and have them ready in case there is a need for more stuff.

Bess

P.S. If you get the stuff from Pat Cullinan the story entitled "Where is the Hour of the Beautiful dancing of Birds," etc has some words missing or misspelt.

1. One line reads — "I am terror-stricken of you of them ..." It should be — I am terror-stricken of him of them...

2. Missing word — "it waves a glittering sword in your face and you fall back, swaying for one awful minute..." N.B. "fall" is left out.

3. Misspelt word. The line reads — ... all a dark flowering silence... it should be — ... all a dark flowing silence...

[12]

P.O. Box 130, Serowe
1 February 1966

Dear Randolph,

The critics are quite true about the writing. On the one hand I never felt I could write about people in S. Africa because they were all torn up and un-representative of any definite kind of wholeness. On the other I find this sympathetic wholeness here but tend to reflect my own condition which is one of unbelievable isolation. Apart from that I'm none too happy in a tribal society. It's VERY repressed. It hasn't a flexibleness to allow for a flow of ideas, activity. People on the whole are quite, quite flat and only here and there you'll get a SPARK. Thought is *en masse* and you struggle to pick out SOME-THING in the blur. But what has been good for me here is as I said pulling my own threads together. I'm not so terribly stuck. Just want to broaden out.

Just at the same time to-day I got a letter from UNO head-quarters. They say they got word from NUSAS [National Union of South African Students] and are considering me for

a training programme and will let me know their decision
soon.

Bess

[13]

Bamangwato Development Association,
Radisele, P.O. Palapye
17 February 1966

Dear Randolph,

Am just leaving for the above address to work as odd job
man on the farm. AM going to write. Will EXTERNALISE. If
I can get to grips with this godforsaken country then nothing
will ever defeat me again. How's that for optimism?
Authorities approved of my stay at the farm. I'm still SUR-
PRISED. Will write again.

Bess

Howard is alright.

[14]

Bamangwato Development Association,
Radisele, P.O. Palapye
4 March 1966

Dear Randolph,

I have decided to take a two year course in agriculture at
this development farm and later work out something for
myself along the lines of food production. Nothing has been
settled yet because I can only stay here if I get a grant. This
seems hopeful as I met the director of the International
University Exchange in Serowe and explained my various

problems to him. I don't know what I can do about Howard and he can at least cope with this country. This farm is an informal place and if I'm not suddenly kicked out I like to stay here for Howard's sake and also the excellent tuition I am likely to get. I enclose a letter written to Dr Opdahl. He is resigning and his place is being taken by Mr Eriksson whom I met in Serowe. Mr Eriksson thought a grant of £300 might tide me over. He said he'd let me know at the end of March. What else can I do? I was feeling pretty desperate in Serowe. The agriculturist is pretty sympathetic and has given me all sorts of jobs already. At the moment I am harvesting Turkish tobacco — which is an experimental venture to see if it could possibly become a cash crop. For the hut I live in I am at the moment doing odd typing jobs but no food is grown because all water has to be reserved for the cattle ranch. The financial situation is pretty, pretty desperate.

I also got a letter from David Machin. He said the same about the stories so asked if I could get started on a full length book. I wrote saying I thought I could but I really must get settled. I feel so harassed and worried. You've no idea what a desolate bundu I've got myself into. Serowe is like Manhattan compared to it. The nearest shop is twenty-five miles away.

I also enclose the reviews. I do hope they are okay. Being so mentally harassed I might have not done as good a job as I ought. Mr Eriksson said he'd try to get me a grant as an exception because they only give grants to people who are prepared to go to university and I'd still have to take matric. I would be forty by the time I got through that: that's why I thought I'd work out something for myself here. Please can you put me on the subscription list of *The New African* and get an invoice sent? I am disastrously cut off at the moment.

Sincerely,
Bessie

[15]

Bamangwato Development Association,
Radisele, P.O. Palapye
22 March 1966

Dear Randolph,

You know what a battle-scarred warrior is like? After some time he just longs for peace — NO MORE FIGHTING. Perhaps in the end there is just coldness and cynicism left. I just keep smiling and talking but I don't love people. They've got a brilliant young man here — Vernon Gibberd. He's wasted here. The farm is managed by an illiterate old man. People can't help themselves. Black people are terribly insecure and this insecurity is shockingly destructive; perhaps without meaning to be. A job; authority; means everything but most of all the pleasure of power over other people. Everybody's got to be somebody's victim because most of the time you're a good little yes-man to some big guy.

There's the possibility of a tremendous communist build-up in this country and it's a big draw for the insecure man who, God help him, is vicious. They've got this lovely young man with big wide innocent eyes and terrific energy and he's slowly being screwed to death by a vicious old man. They're not going to use me to fix in another screw. There's all this talk about helping poor people. Poor illiterate people are cogs in the wheels and given authority, they indulge in a reign of terror. It's going to take years and years for enough schools to be built. And in the meantime you have to be screwed to death by people who can't help themselves. I've had enough of it. I want to do useful work but I'm not Jesus Christ to suffer laceration too.

I might get help from UNO or Leiden to get to Kenya. I can

start differently. Perhaps I can start somewhere there. More slowly, carefully and NO MORE HEART ON THE SLEEVE BUSINESS!! Just sorry for Gibberd. Saw everything here through his eyes. He is just like my blood brother only an innocent person full of glowing idealism. He makes you feel the world can be changed overnight. It's one thing to be an idealist but fatal to be so innocent. He can't even see that people hate him because he's brilliant and they're not and his brilliance offends them.

I feel so ill and frightened, Randolph, because the things essential to my survival — like generosity and a rich flow of ideas — I can't seem to find.

Bessie

[16]

Bamangwato Development Association,
Radisele, P.O. Palapye
14 May 1966

Dear Randolph,

You are my everlasting friend. It's so difficult for me to make out your illegible handwriting!!

I enclose a letter. It's just almost 100% that India will be an opening for me. Actually I don't think I've told you but quite a lot of my previous incarnations were spent in India. When I found this out some time ago I thought deeply about the matter. Actually I'm not the kind of person that's just born for being born sake. It's very significant that I've been born in Southern Africa. All these years I've been trying to find the purpose in it and true enough there's smoke all around but bless me if I can find the fire. I know you are going to think that perhaps adversity has unhinged my mind but its true enough a change has come over me. I've suddenly got the firm conviction that something like the equivalent of God is around in Southern Africa. It's one thing to have the strangest revelations all of a sudden thrust upon one's conscious mind and it's another not to be able to confirm this in reality.

I even said to myself: "B. Head, take care. You've been sitting alone for three months in the desolate wilderness, that's why you've started 'seeing' things."

I'm not quite gone round the bend yet, Randolph, but one or two things will happen: — 1. the unexpected ... or 2. I'll soon get on opening in India.

I've a feeling the unexpected is about to happen but although I've had a lot of the strangest revelations recently I really don't know what to expect. Only thing. I'm feeling on top of the world.

Figure it out — I might have really gone round the bend. I mean people who get visions and see a gigantic light descend on them from the sky can't be all there but if so I feel mighty happy. If one is happy and cracked it's much better than being unhappy and sane.

Don't be alarmed. I haven't developed four horns or six hands. I'm just telling you that all is not what it seems. And I don't know what to expect.

Bechuanaland's a pretty unfathomable country. Oh, one thing. The communists are preparing for a big shoot up here over independence. Perhaps some interesting things will happen. I'll try and see if there's anyone who can cover the independence celebrations for you. Did you ask Pat van Rensburg? He KNOWS everything and he knows what can be said and not said. He's the safest person.

In one half of me I say it would be a good thing if I could get out of here alive with my child. I'd put everything out of my mind and ask for citizenship in India. It's one of the most tolerant countries on earth. I fear it. I fear the violent crosscurrents of hate and fear. There are too many obstructionists and they're black people mind you. That's the difficulty. You can't tell friend from foe and often an apparent foe is a friend. You live on tenterhooks and have to be sharply alert. I told Pat Cullinan — the real battle is going to be between black man and black man. It so pleases destiny to work out progress like that. I somehow think there's going to be no bloodshed here. But I'm terribly alert and I said: "Well damn it — whatever will be will be."

Just know — there's quite a likelihood I might be popped off too. This letter will be opened and read and it's anybody's guess what the openers-of-letters have in mind.

Bess

[17]

c/o P.O. Palapye
2 July 1966

Dear Randolph,

Thank you for your letter. I am at the moment homeless and stranded in Palapye. The committee that runs the farm had many complaints about my living in the visitors' hut. I left the farm on Thursday. My luggage is at the Palapye station.

I don't know what's going to happen but it would be a relief to be free of malice, intrigue and unfathomable, weird, weird people who are shockingly cruel. I'll write to Eriksson with your suggestion. Please help me in whatever way you can. I'm holding on.

Bessie

[18]

P.O. Box 130, Serowe
19 July 1966

Dear Randolph,

Got me a job to-day as a typist for a big road contractor. Going to live out in the bush. He is building the 36 mile road from Palapye to Serowe so I have opened my P.O. Box in Serowe again. It's a god send. They've been looking for someone with INTELLIGIBLE ENGLISH to handle important correspondence. They just rushed me into the job and I've taken it because I'm frightened. Was sheltered for some time by telephone exchange lady at Palapye, who saw me sitting outside P.O. STRANDED. Typing is bad but hope I'll learn. Job is GOOD. Oh God, relief to be employed.

Bess

P.S. English is dubious too. Have to get a DICTIONARY.

[19]

c/o Peter Sladden & Co. Pty. Ltd, P.O. Box 49, Palapye
27 July 1966

Dear Randolph,

I had to change my address again because there are no off times on Saturday and Sunday so I'll have to receive my mail through the above address. Temporarily I am happy here. It's much easier for me to get on with crowds of men (about 200 here) and a very mixed crew from all parts of Southern Africa — Angola, Windhoek, Rhodesia, S. Africa, etc. The road is a vast project, actually 33 miles and only expected to be complete in July next year. That is how long this job ought to last me —- if I'm lucky. I don't know how much salary I'll be receiving but it won't be much. I'm only relieved to have a place to stay and something to do and what I'm doing or associated with is tremendously exciting.

I had no idea that road building was so fascinating. This road is only being built to gravel level. The Government is only spending vast sums on three key roads. One has been built already by the above company from Gaborone to Zeerust border (17 miles) the other is from Palapye to Serowe (33 miles). The other contract, the 183 mile road from Nata to Maun, went to another company. Work goes on here night and day with gigantic machinery-tournapulls, Fordson tractors and the D7 caterpillars. At least, if they won't let me stay in Bechuanaland, I'll be the only woman who was a part of one of the most exciting projects in this country and so it is. I'm the only woman member of the staff in the bush. I have a small slap-dash house, very roughly built with a room and a kitchen.

The business world is thoroughly strange to me. I type out reams of letters quibbling over small sums of money or perhaps I have a mad boss. Oh Lordy I like this atmosphere. There's a lot of good lusty swearing and yelling and no one dreams of calling anyone insane. There's fights too and rough words and blood-curdling threats but soon the storms blow over. I really fit in and am just thinking how I can organise myself in future so that I spend the rest of my life with rough loud swearing men. I don't like hypocrisy and pretence and malice and there's really none of it here. Everybody works hard and they're travellers.

I can't get a scholarship to study as I'm not suitably qualified. Good-bye for now. Soon the boss will come in and find me typing a personal letter and fire me.

Yours as ever, Bessie

P.S. You must not be troubled if my views on God are strange ones. Also please transfer my *New African* to the above address.

[20]

c/o Peter Sladden & Co. Ltd., P.O. Box 49, Palapye
9 August 1966

Dear Randolph,

Thank you for your letter. Did you get the review I sent about 2 weeks ago? It was posted for me by a passing lorry driver and I had difficulty explaining to him how to put on the stamp because he did not understand English. Machin also wrote to me and said the *New Statesman* had accepted one of my short stories and would pay me about £30 for it. He also sent me the galley proof to correct, which I did and returned to him.

It is true I have NOT received the IUEF letter about New Zealand and Lars Eriksson has not written to me for some time. I'm sorry if I wrote L. life letters but I think I've been so miserable that everything's been going round and round in my head. Also the Institute to which I had applied in India turned me down on the grounds that I do not have enough qualifications. Naomi Mitchison, the writer, says I should give up trying to get a scholarship to study agriculture and concentrate on writing something pretty soon which would be solid enough to be published. I told Machin I would try something and I don't feel so hard-pressed and half-crazy now that I have a job. It lasts for a year until next June/July when the road will be complete. Sladden won't take me to his office in Zambia as I am not upper-class enough. I'm just a stop-gap here. My salary is very small, only R30/£15 per month because I am not a qualified typist but I work damn hard and his business is complicated involving much work on the tabular bar and reams of figure work and he wants it done as speedily as possible. But I'm so grateful to have somewhere to stay and food to eat that I've earned that I'm really recovering and feeling very gay.

Solly Ndlovu, PAC representative, wrote to me yesterday. He is in Francistown and he said he could fix all arrangements to get me to Zambia and arrange while still here for a work permit. Matthew [Nkoana] in Cairo told him to help me. I asked him to send me an application form for a work permit. I certainly can't stay in Bechuanaland once this job is through as I somewhat underestimated my enemies and I think I'm not liked because perhaps people do not want to be truthful about their aims.

It's no use me coming to England at great speed and being a liability to people. There is a bit of time now to arrange things, I mean I could see that it would work financially so that I do not have to borrow money from people again. There is nothing more humiliating in the world especially if one is fit and in order and capable of doing a hard job but finds oneself a beggar.

Well I hope this letter has been FACTUAL enough. I don't think I could write about Bechuanaland Independence. I hate it temporarily.

Please don't think I'm writing about life but perhaps I'm not the only person who can't make it in Africa. I'd hate to think I'm solo perhaps I'd be lost anywhere else but it's been Batswana people I've been fighting with, so God help me, and that does not endear me to anyone, especially as I'm some kind of half-caste. You've no idea how frightened I really am because I thought Africa was my home and now I don't know what to do.

Bessie

How do you write about nothing. You must make yourself a part of the life of the country, even if it's painful and confused and people struggle for their own expression in a maybe brutal and cruel manner, because of the inferiority complex.

[21]

Bamangwato Development Association,
Radisele, P.O. Palapye
[no date]

Dear Randolph,

I was fired from the typing job for Sladden on Friday. Can't explain except that the circumstances were very sordid. Seems if I decide to sleep with every Tom, Dick and Harry — I'll keep a job.

I've joined the refugees here and registered myself under PAC to go to Zambia — God knows when. I'm not blaming anybody.

Bessie

If anyone can help me to leave Africa I'd be grateful. I don't want to and will never be allowed to live anywhere without being hounded by unscrupulous men who think women are cheap.

After the end of her teaching post in Serowe, there was our attempted rescue operation, then her brief period on the farm at Radisele (which provided so much of *When Rain Clouds Gather*, just as the germ of *Maru* is in letters 1 and 4), the even briefer time with the road construction firm near Palapye, ending in "circumstances [that] were very sordid" one year after her first letter to me. These were the times of her struggle to put together enough of her stories and sketches to make a book. But it was a book that no one wanted, and all that came from it were the stories and reviews in *The New African*, the short-lived *African Review*, *Classic*, *Transition*, and the War on Want journal. The last, I fancy, was through early contact with Betty Sleath, an elderly lady, once a farmer but now leading a Spartan existence in an Ealing bed-sit and giving all her time to War on Want. Betty was perhaps the most faithful admirer of us all.

Some of the stories may have appeared later under different titles. I do not know the fate of "Earth Love" and "Beautiful Dancing of Birds." Bessie's great leap forward, the appearance in the *New Statesman* of "The Woman from America" was in August 1966. Publishers and agents began to look at her work, but only Keith Sambrook at Heinemann and David Machin, who left Heinemann to join Gregson & Wigan as an agent at that time, took at all seriously this intense and rather unfathomable young woman out in remote Botswana.

Sambrook wrote of her "definite talent" but found her writing "too undisciplined and introverted." He urged that she externalise her feelings and embody them in her characters. "But she can definitely *write* [his emphasis] and should be encouraged." His letter to me reads patronizingly today, but it was unusually positive from a London publisher dealing with an unknown African author at that time. It was good to be able to transmit this view, which she duly registered, promising to "externalise" as she set off for Radisele.

David Machin's first letter (which he copied to me) must

have reached her at the farm near Radisele in the Bamangwato area. He warned her that "South African fiction is on the whole poorly supported here by the public and, if it is of any great worth, usually banned in South Africa itself, as you know, so publishers have great difficulty in finding a market for it." Short stories were particularly hard to place. He suggested she write a book "on what is happening in Bechuanaland ... how it is affecting tribal society." The growing pile of stories she had submitted were sent to Mark Bonham-Carter at Collins, to whom I had put Bessie's case. He deplored the end of short-story publishing and also asked for a Bechuanaland book. My attempts to get to Machin the novel written in Cape Town, which Bodley Head had rejected in 1963, came to naught, as it was with a publisher in South Africa. I believe the manuscript is now with Patrick Cullinan.

For all her "odd solitary way of living," Bessie soon recruited a corps of friends and well-wishers at home and abroad, with whom she kept in close touch except when at her nadir. A few were from her South African days, some valued her as a writer of promise, but most were more concerned with her as a refugee, a vulnerable and lonely figure, with her small child and absence of means or a residence permit. The centre of these was Patrick van Rensburg. His letters assert how unwelcome was his role, heavily burdened as he was during the infancy of Swaneng Hill School, which he had founded in 1963, and Bessie does not always treat him fairly in hers. Like some others, he was unwilling to be drawn into time-consuming arguments and discussions with Bessie. He found specially unwelcome her hostile attitude to local society. This put him on his guard, since "one suspects that people are trying to catch one out when they do this." With all his struggles to fulfil his dream for Botswana — and Africa — he found time, sometimes money, to help. She repaid some of his quiet, constant support in *Serowe: Village of the Rain Wind* (1977).

A more mobile supporter was Naomi Mitchison, who had been appointed by their Chief, Bathoen, "mother" of the Bakgatla, and who came and went, bringing first-hand news. She replied to Bessie in *The New African* (March 1966) with an article "For Serowe: a capital city". Patrick van Rensburg's conscience, she wrote," drove him out of a life of comfort and status in his native South Africa, to come with his Welsh wife and found a school at Serowe. It was history to have two whites living in a rondavel, teaching in a shed, the wife cooking and washing — and teaching ... If, three years ago, anyone had said how wonderfully Swaneng Hill School would grow and prosper, nobody would have believed them." Yet Bessie was blind to Patrick's contribution and achievement. Her perspective was very different. She had not sacrificed comfort and status but looked back to the life summed up in the early pages of *A Question of Power*, to a childhood spent "sitting under a lamp-post near her house, crying because everyone was drunk and there was no food, no one to think about children."

Naomi Mitchison, prolific novelist, biographer and critic, grande dame and matriarch, sister of J.B.S.Haldane, wife of a Labour peer, yet found time to write a profile of Bessie in *The Guardian* in 1967. She called the half-finished *Rain Clouds* "a book of immense understanding of the Batswana," and reported that Bessie, though "one of the many hapless people without proper papers ... now has a typewriter and a little confidence and the knowledge that a few of us are backing her for a winner." She predicted "it will take another generation, perhaps, before she is 'discovered' and becomes someone whom people will proudly remember having seen in the grim streets of Francistown."

Those others, known to me, who tried to help Bessie fulfil her farming ambition, her writer's destiny or to move out of Botswana, I can do little more than list: Cato Aall, Canon John Collins (the always open-handed founder of Christian Action and Defence & Aid), Lars-Gunnar Eriksson (before the calamitous infiltration of the International University Exchange Fund by the South African police spy Williamson), Terence Finley, Vernon Gibberd (the Gilbert of *Rain Clouds*), Tim Holmes (a *New African* founder who had moved to Zambia), Martin and Mary Kibblewhite at Swaneng, Margaret Legum, Bridget Mellor, and Bessie's ex-husband Harold, whom she much traduced to others. There were plans for her to move to Britain, India, Israel, Kenya, Norway, Sweden, the United States and

41

Zambia. These resettlement plans ran concurrently and the planners were often unaware of each other's existence. Shocks were not uncommon, as in Harold's letter to me from Lincoln University in January 1966, telling me that Bessie had just written, in December, that she was "leaving for West Germany the following week to take up a scholarship and 'eventually marry' a pen friend of five years' standing." The pen friend was not heard of again.

"The Woman from America" changed all that. The *New Statesman* was still a major literary and political weekly and the article brought a flood of answers to her simple question: "Would someone please write me an explanation of what a machine tool is? I'd like to know. My address is Serowe, Bechuanaland, Africa." A fellow writer from New York told her "I am not any more certain of what a machine tool is than you are," but put Bessie in touch with one of her most distinguished South African fellow-countrymen, Dr Z.K. Matthews, who was about to become Botswana's first Ambassador to the United Nations, and with his son Knox, on his way from Birmingham to a medical post in Botswana. The corps of friends became a small army and it began to seem as if that lifeline to London was less needed than before, an impression soon to be dispelled.

2. Francistown
15 January 1966 – 14 January 1969

[22]

P.O. Box 207, Francistown, Botswana
4 October 1966

Dear Randolph,

I wrote you a short filler on Independence. If it's useful you can use it. A personal bit piece. I haven't a typewriter yet.

Bessie

P.S. United Nations offered me a scholarship to Tanzania. They also applied to Botswana govt. for a one way stateless person's document. If they refuse they've also made the same application to the Zambian govt. and Tanzanian govt. I hear this takes months to negotiate.

[23]

P.O. Box 207, Francistown
29 October 1966

Dear Randolph,

Thank you for the postcard. It is quite all right to send the six copies of *The New African*. I shall make some arrangements here. Francistown is much more sophisticated and "civilised" than the rest of Botswana.

Funny thing. David Machin sent me a copy of the *New*

Statesman with my story and you say you sent one as well. Neither reached me. I just wonder if the powers that be are offended about that remark I passed about the State Department, America.

Really, I am full of anxiety. Frankly, the last thing I am ever going to do is re-settle myself in ANY African state. Botswana is tolerable to me because up till now Authority is reasonable. Policemen aren't over-anxious to arrest and shove people around. There's an over-all feeling of normality and not much bossism. But anywhere else, I shall be mangled in a day, particularly Tanzania. Why should Nyerere force young people into military training? We aren't really going to make it as war-mongers. The worst possible thing a government can do is to persecute young people.

My plan is this. I shall just have to get SOMETHING written. While I am here. And I am prepared to strain every nerve, day and night to write the best, I've ever written. There is no alternative. After that I might be in a position to by-pass ANY circumstance; any revolution in Africa where the individual is an expendable commodity. If it means raising my own cash to be a useful person somewhere then I would rather do that. But I can't be shoved around by pompous fools. I haven't a vendetta of hate. Quite the opposite.

It is no exaggeration to say that in Botswana I learnt tolerance, love, brotherhood because that is what is in the air here. And I want to affirm clearly what I have learnt here, because it seems important to me. But I do not think I shall survive in any other part of Africa and I am not prepared to try.

Peter Mackay, who is in Zambia and is responsible for clearing refugees out of Botswana, wrote saying that it would be some time before the Zambian govt. decided to clear me. I did not meet Margaret Legum [then Secretary of the Joint Committee on the High Commission Territoreis]

44

because I am not staying at the camp and since I had a row with the PAC fellows here no one informed me. When I arrived, apart from trying to force me by the hair to sleep with him, J wanted to stuff some idiotic literature and attitudes down my throat. I let him have a piece of my mind and ever since then I have been treated as a spy or something untouchable. He said he was going to denounce me as "a PAC adventurer and a useless person in the struggle." No doubt he has; that is why I think the Zambian govt. won't give me clearance and in any case I am *sick* of silly, dishonest people.

I am determined to survive. Because of Howard. I got him into this ghastly mess. And if writing can open some doors of dignity and respect which I so badly need; then I shall very soon open up a way for myself.

Dr Matthews, who is at present in Francistown told me that England is a FREE country. Also I have a real friend, there, a writer, who wrote to me after my story was published in the N.S. Her name is K. In fact I have lots of people writing to me from all over the world now, even Singapore. Its not so hopeless. I am only strained beyond endurance and impatient with any system of government that destroys mankind.

Mr R. Phahle said the minimum requirements for a teaching post in England is matric. I told him I am only a J.C. and asked him to find out if a J.C. plus two year teaching course would be acceptable.

As ever,
Bessie

P.S. Would you like to get in touch with my friend K? She has written something on the African scene but she did not explain what.

[24]

P.O. Box 207, Francistown
25 January 1967

Dear Randolph,

Just to-day I received a Christmas card from you and Gillian for which I thank you both very much. I also received the December issue of *The New African* in which Naomi Mitchison lammed me again for calling Francistown a town. On the piece of paper which covered *The New African* was a note which said: Look here, I'm very busy. So I took it that you did not want me to write to you about my usual complaints on life and the universe. This letter, then, isn't to you but to ask you to pass it on to someone who might be interested in helping me with a few contributory ideas for a scheme I have in mind.

Pass it on. Here goes: In December Simon & Schuster, an American publishing firm, advanced me eighty pounds to get busy on a book. In fact I had already started on Chapters 1 & 2 and the book is called *When Rain Clouds Gather*. Machin has already read the first two chapters and he says: I think they are very good indeed. The whole thing is set at a development project, where I actually lived for five months but I want to go beyond what was going on there which was NOTHING. Simon & Schuster also have Chapters 1 & 2 and I am still waiting to hear from them and no doubt I shall be in a fix because it has people in it quite identifiable. 19,000 words are already done.

Part of the book covers the severe drought of last year in which 600,000 cattle died and even this year people can't plough, those who use oxen, because of this heavy loss.

I have a theme, towards the end of my book. In a country

like this no talent or intelligence should go to waste. I want to set out the framework in which this ideal could be fulfilled and the setting is there ready made: the development farm where I stayed [The Bamangwato Development Association was founded by Chief Tshekedi Khama and Guy Clutton-Brock. The experimental farm it ran at Radisele is described briefly in *Serowe: Village of the Rain Wind* by Vernon Gibberd, "Gilbert" of *Rain Clouds*] but in the book I give it another name and a different inspirer. I also have the individual in mind who could bring this kind of scheme to a living reality and it is he about whom the book is written ... and who I am going to let read the manuscript .... In any case I began to understand a lot of things: —

1. A kind of organisation could be started where everyone could come and learn something.

2. There is a vast amount of knowledge and help available and how to bring this knowledge and people together. Especially young people, of Botswana.

3. This would be the kind of place where drought problems were studied; developing drought resistant seeds and the ways and means of finding new and cheaper sources of fuel to get machinery, etc., moving.

What outline would one need to get something like this started? The people are there but how to make all this coherent? I chose a two-way theme — I have the views of the man right down below and how he survives and how a Cambridge educated man looks at this. These are the twin themes of the book. But I have to work this towards a strong conclusion and I find myself a little restricted as far as getting hold of what I need, though the will and imagination are there and in a poetic speculative way I did involve myself in the hunger and famine of this country. In the end I want this to be handled by a person — not governments

47

and committees because they bugger everything up.

Bessie

I kept the letter short but for anyone interested I could quote parts of my book.

Could you send me the November issue of *The New African* with my story — "Chibuku Beer and Independence." Where is Harold Head? He asked me to divorce him.

I may be leaving Botswana at the end of Feb. on UNO scholarship but they are still looking for a country for me.

[25]

P.O. Box 207, Francistown
10 February 1967

Dear Randolph,

Thank you for your letter of 1st Feb. I am so relieved that you did not write that odd note on the wrapper. It might have been one of the folks in the office. Most of the time I do not trust myself to write sane letters to people, so I am always on the look-out for when I have caused offence.

About Pat's school and Pat. Pat isn't a get-to-know kind of person, but, he can't stand it when anybody from South Africa gets into a mess here and a lot of black South Africans do, for one reason and another. Most of the African countries abide by things and subtle forms of fear etc and we have lost this, but it gets at you still and at some time or other you get into a fix. When this happens and Pat gets to know of it, he sticks his neck out. Just at the time you are entangled in a net of weird happenings. Not only me, but quite a lot of others have been helped like this. For my own self he raised a total of two-hundred pounds which he gave me in lots of three pounds a week, until I came here and went on the refugee dole. Well during the time everybody in Serowe said I was a crazy person, all the volunteers from his school started coming over to my hut. And then asking me over to the school and at that time I had been thinking of what to do next and I was amazed at what was going on there. You have the school on one side and a hundred village development projects on the other. Communal owned vegetable gardens, supervised by a biologist. Builders' brigades, cooking and sewing for adult women ... Actually there is a long catalogue of works going on there because a lot of the OXFAM aid money went to the school. I myself wrote to Liz [van Rensburg] about the vegetable garden and in less than two weeks it was started. That's the sort of place Swaneng is, where all sorts of things get started month after month. The other thing is that there is one batch of good folks who won't leave. They keep extending their service because they are so involved. Most of the others come for a year and then go back. The thing is Pat never preaches and few know him yet everybody who is there works with him. A project may start but he keeps in the background, just dishing out the cash and in some queer way keeping things going. He is also very close to Seretse Khama. I think they are real buddies and I think that Seretse Khama is the surprise of Africa. You know something? During those years of being in the background he made the most experiments in farming in Botswana. And he sets the tone for a government that is after economic security. But that's how far I got because I know little and few people.

What this book I'm writing is all about. Last December [1966] Pat invited me for Christmas lunch and into the dining room walked one of the most interesting individuals on earth. The drought was raging at that time and the cattle were dying and he kept talking about Botswana as though it was an obsession with him. So I found out that he was working at the farm which was started by Tshekedi and Clutton Brock. I lived there for five months, driven half crazy by a Batswana manager of the farm who was married to some first relative of Tshekedi. At first the Batswana manager sort of stipulated that I ought not to like this man because of some long standing feud they had. But I had gone there because I liked the ideas of the man and that was the only reason. And he had written reams on Botswana agriculture and it was all of a sorting-out nature and how he had fitted himself into the position of very poor people. All this appealed to me while the Batswana man did not because being up in this royal family thing he despised poor people. So I collected all sorts of bits of information about agriculture and wrote little notes on wild flowers and all the pretty and amazing side of Botswana life. Then the farm committee asked me to leave. When I got to Francistown I started putting them together into book form working almost day and night. 30,000 words done so far.

I sent 5,000 words of the book to Simon & Schuster and one of their editors sort of adopted me and even sent me a ream of typing paper. Luck is just there but most times my heart fails me because of the type of thing I am writing. Polythene pit dams are being built, and an old man expresses his views about what it is like to be poor and how a poor man thinks. Very few characters and the going is hard. Also the publishers complained that the male narrator sounds like a woman and they asked me to change everything to the third person, to widen out the range and horizon. The sort of ending I had in mind is a mustard seed because I thought that this man who had an obsession about Botswana might be genuine and a book like this might help him. So I do thank you for the names and addresses. Especially the T.B. one. In the fact sheet on Botswana, T.B. is listed as the main killer. All that one puts it down to is inadequate diet, mabele with a dash of meat day in and day out. And sometimes just mabele. And sometimes just god-all nothing. I've been through this too. And the awful mud huts which cause pneumonia, the next major killer.

K is a wonderful woman ... She always gives me advice on how to be a great writer but I can only accomplish what I can and I can just push myself so far. And the good lord knows I am in pain about what I'm doing now because I've been given a little money for it and am therefore under the gun to come up with the goods. The thought of being a great writer just does not appeal to me right now. It makes me feel sick and I feel too frightened to think of all the little petty decisions and refugee rumours that are life to me now. One of the rumours is that I don't stand a chance of getting permanent residence in Africa because I was a state witness in 1960 about a case in which a letter had been found in my possession. And the book doesn't say pretty things about tribal people. Those at the top. But what is below is good, if it gets the chance to live.

Sincerely, Bessie

[26]

P.O. Box 207, Francistown
11 December 1967

Dear Randolph,

I was pleased to receive your letter too. Not having heard from you for so long, I did not dare write, thinking you might have moved to a new address or got lost. Then *The New African* arrived about a month ago and I still did not write. It was lovely of David Machin to tell you about the book .(More

51

about the book and *The New African* later). I was grieved to read of the death of Pat Duncan in the papers. If there was ever a truthful man, with courage, he was one. It's terrible where truth and courage may lead one. I don't know how this came about but some PAC member said in reply to a remark of mine that I admired that man — "Oh he's a sell out." So, on the day I read in the papers that Pat was dead, I was standing in the shop with this person and turned on him in a wild burst of rage — "Aren't you glad the sell out is dead? Aren't you glad now? You bloody bastards can rest in peace because you have no more sell outs."

I want you to do me a favour, Randolph. If my book is to be reviewed in the *New African* will you please do it and not give it to anyone else. I think you will grasp what the hero of my book, Makhaya, is suffering about. He is the sort of fellow who can't go along with all the swines in the name of African liberation and because of this I picked mainly on the supporters of Pan Africanism to show up the kind of things they really do and which I have seen with my own eyes. You know, in the bible, there was this fellow, Solomon, who was so grand and who taxed the people heavily for his gold candlesticks. I called the fellows of the liberatory struggle, aspiring Solomons and Makhaya who goes to a farm and does a real job or work is, in their language, a traitor to the African cause. There were many things I debated and had to give way to due to my circumstances and also the position in which I put Makhaya in the book. I made the suffering of a black man personal and towards the end I got so confused I just had to say that there was a God behind it all and even now I blow hot and cold and wring my hands in agony the way Makhaya does throughout the book. You can look at it with a balanced eye. I brought a British volunteer into it and I have had such terrible dreams. One night I dreamt someone said to me: "This book will be read with great acclaim next year but you will achieve your success at the expense of Pan Africanism." And it was so vivid because I turned to the person in great distress and quoted a line from my book ... "To many, Pan Africanism is a sacred dream, but like all dreams it also has its nightmare side and the doings of the little men like Joas Tsepe are the nightmare ..."

Now in the book I imply certain things. A man must have a backbone and he must observe some moral standards and Makhaya reaches these conclusions through his own suffering and not by paying lip service to what I call "all the fashionable ideologies."

I did note the letter of Stokely Carmichael in *The New African*. First of all I think it has shot up to being one of the best magazines in Africa and secondly I like the way in which it makes everything admissible because this is necessary. It is necessary to tell the truth as people feel it and Stokely Carmichael is just as much admissible as Martin Luther King. (For one thing, Negro people can't take it anymore, all the hypocrisy and the slap on the one cheek and turning the other. But they won't join the Black Muslims because the Black Muslims say they must not eat pork and this is the favourite Sunday dish of Negro people in America. Then this feeling of "I can't take it anymore," still comes out in fellows like Stokely. I don't know if he's a black Muslim but he looks a handsome young fellow and good soap box orator from the picture I saw of him — like Tom Mboya.)

Personally, the feeling of rage and hard lump of fury inside is like an electric wire that snaps and just runs wild. I have found such people may have a far deeper hate for their fellow black man than they do for the white man and this dumbfounds me. I was friends for more than a year here with a Negro woman, whom I wrote about in the *New Statesman*.

Well, she had an unending list, so to speak, of people who had to be shot, and they were all black people who were traitors to the African or Afro-American cause. I'm afraid I'm on the list! There's something wrong, Randolph. The hate whips back and devours the most unexpected people. I used to listen to this in agony and shake like a jelly fish with fright. Then there's this screwball, Martin Luther King. He's the kind of man who takes the most mental buffeting because he attempts to set himself astride too many wild fires. The truth is, you see the real enemy and how brutal he is — how brutal and evil it is to hate people for just being born. If there were anything else other than the black man's looks and his pitch black skin colour like mid-night — but the deep truth is that he is abhorred and detested for looking different and for too long he's been the circus ape who knew nothing. People like Stokely want to assert the right of this black skin to live on earth. I feel once this is established there will be only social problems left. I begin to feel this way about Africa, and its tribalism. It's a social problem and not the peculiarity of the Black man. This or that is social and every man, throughout the world, has an environment not much to his liking.

Martin Luther King days: "All hatred is bad." Boris Pasternak says: "People can only be drawn to goodness by goodness." The truth is I get inclined to this at times but then I clearly see and feel that this is not the full explanation. There are really wicked people on this earth. BUT THEY ARE NOT IN CAMPS. Therefore you can't say all communists and supporters of communism are good. The most evil people are there. Therefore you can't say all white men are evil. The most good people are found there side by side with terrible brutes. You can't say, African people, because they walk around in rags and tatters, are good. Here, in this continent you just get the extremes — the extremes of kindness and generosity and the extremes of the most terrible evil. In the end you just wring your hands in agony, to prevent you from harming your fellow men — for you do not know whom it is you harm. It may be your own God. And deeper, beyond this is a sort of terrible, roaring fire. When it touches your life, you become quite still with shock. You really then begin to want to depend on some guidance, from somewhere because you feel we are all victims of a strange, concealed destiny. I mean, I could have been born a white man. I have no control over it. I shake with terror at the thought. Say, some merciful fate put me on the receiving side of brutality and ignorance, but what if I were born to mete this out to others? I don't think any black man suffers as much as a white man — his torments and fears must be terrible and the man who is at the receiving end is actually strengthened, while he is weakened and weakened and weakened, day by day. This shout of rage of Mr Stokely Carmichael is a shout from the depths of the deep, true exultant power he is receiving by being the man down there. It's a kind of power that leaps up from the feet to the head in a drunken ecstasy. I feel Mr Stokely does not know this. He might fall down on his knees and glorify his enemy. I feel these things go on in the subconscious and we give them the wrong names, and even when we try to explain them like Martin Luther, we don't reach the depths.

Yours sincerely,
Bessie

[27]

P.O. Box 207, Francistown
28 March 1968

Dear Randolph,

Just a day past I received the No. 50 issue of *The New African*.

What I saw inside caused me to say to myself: "Ha, so my everlasting friend, Randolph, has now descended to pinching. He has pinched some parts of a private letter I wrote to him. He must be famished for some of my writing."

I right away sat down and produced an article "Africa & Revolutions" which you may use in your next issue if you please. I cannot bear the thought that you should pinch for lack of material from me.

I also want to make a bargain with you. I owe you for some issues of *The New African*, so please deduct the money from this article. Also, you said you had sent me a copy of an article I wrote on Botswana Independence. This article, which was in that issue of *The New African* was pinched by the Batswana authorities. They are always doing that when I write anything on Botswana. Therefore the article "Chibuku Beer" never reached me.

Now we shall have to make a careful move to get that issue to me. It was somewhere late 1966. Could you please find a spare copy in the office? Please don't send me the whole magazine because they will somehow smell it and pinch it again. Please cut out "Chibuku Beer and Independence" and send it to me registered, air mail. I think you will be able to afford this as I'm sure I don't owe you very much for past issues of *The New African*.

Also, I profoundly mistrust your absent-mindedness. Put

this letter in your pocket. Take it to the office. Cut out "Chibuku Beer." Send it to me registered air mail.

At the time I wrote "Chibuku Beer" I was unable to make a copy having few writing materials. I thought about it and wanted to re-examine some of the sentiments I expressed about Botswana as against what I feel now. I have noticed that I've often said things unconsciously and then come to feel deeply about them at a later date.

Yours sincerely,
Bessie

[28]

P.O. Box 207, Francistown
2 April 1968

Dear Randolph,

No, I don't think you could be boastful or self-pitying. What I had always taken in you to be common sense and sanity, seems these days to be tinged with humility, too. Perhaps there are many kinds of humilities in this world but I mean the one a person acquires in "deafening silence, headaches and lack of support."

I thank you very much for "Chibuku Beer." It amazes me that it got through the censors. Also your letter arrived in record time. They usually keep it a week or two and I'm not quite sure who is so interested in your correspondence but I suspect it's Botswana because I've been away so long from South Africa. I would not mind if you could now send me the whole issue and risk them removing it. Also, if it's possible, the issue containing the article: "For Serowe, A Village in Africa."

Don't pay heed to L troubling her head about me. For one

thing there is scarcely any love between us and the woman has some incredible ideas. She thinks H is going to be the Prime Minister of South Africa one day. She says he is the real founder of PAC and not Sobukwe. PAC only rates a thought because of the originality of mind of Sobukwe. I only loved that man. I only love brilliance that's why I fell into that hell of a mess. I love something else too. I like the kind of man you walk into a room and overlook and then the impact of him steals on you slowly. Sobukwe is like that. You discover him for yourself. God, I love anything silent and reserved, nothing flashy and loud and stupid. L does not love me but she picked up some rumours here in Francistown about the complicated happenings in Serowe. They are quite dead now. I don't think I'll leave Botswana, not when so much of my life and thought have gone into it. To-day it's most natural for me to just reel off the development problems of this country. And I'll be living this way for some time. There's things I've found here for my own life that I cannot lose. I like the way I am just a nonentity, a nobody. I like the silence and all the hours I turn to study books or study myself. I like the way I have to walk miles for water and carry it home on my head. And I just like the Batswanas, not the big shots, but all the people who walk around with no shoes.

I have an ambition about this country. I said to myself: The best and most enduring love is that of rejection. The fact that I write the way I do about people here in spite of them having said I was insane, surely proves that this love is real. Because I often forget, I only remember the sunshine. Then I said: I'm going to bloody well adopt this country as my own, by force. I am going to take it as my own family. Then since my ambitions are high I am going to put what I think is finest and noblest in Africa in Botswana and show it as having the best of tribal culture. I am helped in this ambition by many things in the society. There is a tradition here not to steal and kill. There is much more too — the destiny of Southern Africa.

I don't much fancy life in England. I don't want people not to give me the change properly in the shop just because I'm black. But I want to assert black in the right way. I've also got a feeling, something queer and laughable that I can catch hold of God for Africa. I want this God to be something like D. H. Lawrence imagined him, loving women. And taking into account that machinery, agriculture, progress go hand in hand with spiritual knowledge. All these things I can only work out in Botswana. Should people like L get hold of the situation in Southern Africa they will just grab the posh houses for themselves. We will have Nkrumah repeated. But don't tell anyone I don't like them and never intend having them rule all these poor and tattered people in Africa. These are the people I really bow down to. I have learnt to do it here. I say the world is only going one way. That my God will fill the hungry with good things. I liked it when you called my piece — the flies in the tea — because most of the volunteers come over here with my God in mind. Some keep right away in the bush, one at least. He just lives there with all these tattered people and I have written my book about him.

Don't worry that I should ever become swollen-headed. Not by writing. Perhaps I cannot describe to you how I have lived this whole year. I have had to discipline myself to stay a week on end without food. And yet somehow hold my mind together. There have been days and days when I've had to give all the food to my son and then sit up the whole night typing my book. Now and then Naomi sent me ten pounds. Because she loves me to love Botswana . There's nothing like outright hunger over a prolonged period to make you lie back and stare deeply at life. I thought I should grasp this for the future. It does not matter to me what critics say or who pats me on the head. Perhaps I'm even grateful for the little money I am getting from the publishers. Perhaps I am grateful for the loneliness, the indifference and the fact that I had to create my own fire to keep me warm.

The book to be published was written in a terrible, haphazard way. It's very rushed. But out of it will come the next — about the family I now have and it will be slower, more carefully planned. I am trying to steal the thunder and might of the old Jewish testament for Africa. Half of it is here, in the tribe. The God is missing. I have developed an affection for old Jehovah and feel I grasp some of the workings of his mind through the prophets like Samuel and Nathan. But this is still all at my finger tips. I don't know how I'm going to take the dive, just yet. This turning towards the tribe came with what I've written in the first book. I was very anti-tribe there. Anything which held up progress got a sound lashing. I thought that could hold out. But now I want a symphony, something from the depths of a people and I find myself turning to the very thing I tried to destroy.

I am going through something like a torture here and perhaps I want some sound advice from you so that I can avoid a repetition of it. It concerns the type of people who read one's writing and then write to one. Mostly David Machin holds the letters but with the *New Statesman* piece a lot got through. Most people told me how interested they were in African development. Then stopped there. The few who held on are at great pains to inform me in almost every letter of how ignorant I am. A few I managed to shake off by suddenly blowing up and telling them to get to hell but I am trapped, trapped in one of the most painful experiences of my life. It's with K. Whom I asked to meet you. I have no way of breaking off with her without seemingly breaking myself too because of what I might say. Because of all I did not say, throughout this whole year.

K also writes. Not long after she started correspondence with me she ... started on a book. At the time I began writing to her I'd just come to Francistown. The way in which I'd come here and it's causes used to make me live out some weird days, often with the feeling that my neck was broken off from the rest of my body. I kept falling down because my legs used to shake. Then she said: How are you living? So I told her this, about the refugee life and how I'd lost my job in Serowe. With the very next letter she sent me 25 pounds which I straight-away took to a shop here and bought this typewriter. She requested that I pay her back the 25 pounds in my own good time. I was deeply grateful. I took it she had saved my neck from breaking off completely because just at that time I felt I could do all sorts of things with this typewriter and pull myself out of the nightmare. This of course I wrote and told her, also at the same time enclosing a short story which I offered as a present because I had nothing else and did not want to be only on the taking side.

A week later I received a bulky letter from K. Inside was the short story I'd sent her as a gift. Almost all of it was page by page crossed through with a pencil over which she scrawled RUBBISH, RUBBISH. Then the accompanying letter said: You African writers won't make it. The great writers of the world are British, Russian and French. You must read *Moby Dick*. You must read Babel. You live on other people's leavings .... And so the tirade went on and on for almost six pages. As though the lady was quite mad and taken out of herself not knowing what she was saying. At the end of the letter she scrawled a P.S. "I have just phoned Randolph's wife. She says she thinks you can write. I too still think you can make it."

For a few days I did not know how to reply. I felt there was something wrong but a lot of what she said was right. I know I can't hold an emotion at a climax. I pay too little attention to painting in a scene. And then I was also deeply attracted to some of her poetry. She has a very activated style. She puts adjectives down in such a way that they become verbs and yet something new and fresh too. So I said: I'll learn something if I take this. I like this woman's style and I'm short of new approaches. Also I owe her £25 and how can I break with her, though she seems mad?

Therefore I wrote back on this theme: I'll certainly learn something from you. The next letter she says: "I always destroy human relationships. I don't want them to get to be a big thing. I mistrust people."

... So I shied away from open battle. I still had no money to pay her back. Even so I won't fight unless I mean it to be the last ditch and I often don't like the last battle because then I fight to kill. Either you or I die and I don't care who dies, you or I.

So I hit upon a way out. I have some outlandish ideas about God. I started letting her have them, in every letter. At first she sent cautious little enquiries? Yes, you are right about Christ, she said once, but ... I let her have the but too. I was even relieved to have something other than personal to discuss. Then Naomi wrote something about me in *The Guardian* and K got a nervous break down. I kept getting funny letters from her, apologising for her upper middle class upbringing. I shied away from this too.

Then I mentioned, just by the way, only because you told me you were writing to her that my book had been accepted. She said nothing about receiving a letter from you. I was relieved. I went on again about God. In one letter she said: Where's the book? So foolishly I said: The manuscript is temporarily mislaid. Also one contract. She wrote back an ecstatic letter. What will you do now that your book is lost? Are you going to stay there? Are you taking the scholarship? I was appalled. I did not know how to say that David had made a mix up with the first and second drafts and that he had written me a panic-stricken letter and that it was all right now. I just shut up and dived into God again. But I fear the lady will go stark raving mad the day my book is published. She thinks I am inferior to her, intellectually, what do I do? She is good in her own right. I have to write at my level. I want her to leave me alone.

Bessie

P.S. M is queer. I told him so in Cape Town. He ought to find quiet work in an office with figures and statistics.

[29]

P.O. Box 207, Francistown
31 October 1968

Dear Randolph,

You sound so depressed, my everlasting friend. I shall certainly review the books when I receive them and let you have the copy right away. Simon & Schuster said my books will be out early next year in the US. They are sending me some advance copies. I can let you have one through David Machin as he is sure to get some. Everything is through with the publishers. I have done the galley proofs. It's not vast. 60,000 words.

My friend, my heart is as sore as yours is. I cannot write poetry just now. But you won't give up fiddling with the written word so I shall write for you again, after the judgement day. I laugh when I think of that poem you published.

You did not like me then because I was such a hot rod black nationalist. I very soon got over that phase because many people pointed out to me that I was not black enough. I began to feel queer, that something was wrong somewhere and that my destiny led me along other paths. Some people can hog the back skin for themselves but I have to opt for mankind as a whole. You know, my friend, a combination such as I of two nations finally establishes the human race. To tell the truth I am too passionate for that role. I like being a giant of a hell bent track. You used to see how I used to glare, didn't you? Well, the giant is brought down to his knees right now and sweating blood.

It's over Howard. For six years I worked him into a nice little mess. I think I was over-anxious that he have an environment. It was I who told him he was a Motswana and indeed he speaks Setswana fluently. He walked up to Pat van Rensburg's child one day and addressed him in Setswana because that is all the little children speak. No sooner did he go to school, this year than the children at school told him he is a coloured. Apparently being a Motswana is a very exclusive thing. He kept on complaining about this and I used to break out into a sweat not knowing what to say because I started it in the first place. I don't think he understands words like human being and mankind. Eventually he got assaulted by children twice his age, apparently on the grounds that he is an usurper into the race of Motswana, or some filthy specimen. I withdrew him from school because he can't handle such a situation. Neither can I. I frankly don't know what to do, except teach him myself. This is just a temporary measure. I thought I had not figured my own self out. There is something in me that is my own way and very precious. My mother made it that way for me. Because of the way she died. I don't think I told you this but my mother's family locked

64

her up in a mental asylum for sleeping with a black man. I feel they did this to save the family name from scandal and she was in the asylum by the time I was born. I carried this with me for a long time. There is a terrible depth of loneliness in supposed or even evident insanity. There is more. A birth such as I had links me to her in a very deep way and makes her belong to that unending wail of the human heart ... Why? Why? How do I know if she loved my father? She must have been as mad and impulsive as I. She must have loved going at a man and grabbing him around the neck and found white men too stiff for that game. You can only do that to a black man. He just loves it when you go at him and grab him around the neck. I am just like her. I like to do things to men and say all kinds of horrible things and be very provocative. It is a special kind of man who appreciates an impulsive woman. I still say she belongs to me in a special way and that there is no world as yet for what she has done. She left me to figure it out. I feel more for her than my father because she died a terrible death, in a loony bin while he is most probably still alive somewhere. Randolph I am sick at heart just now. The world is really an awful place. I felt that something is going to crack or so, soon. Nothing is too bad for me to experience.

Bessie

[30]

P.O. Box 207, Francistown
12 November 1968

Dear Randolph,

Have just received your short note. Wrote you last week. That bloody woman K nearly killed me. She is a monstrous sucker of one's blood. She only thinks of herself. She wrote me that the article "God and the Underdog" was not so good as the *New Statesman* piece. She's been telling me that the only thing I ever wrote and will ever write is that N.S. piece. I got mad. I said: "Look here, that article is (in the N.A.) greater than the N.S. piece. I wrote it with my heart on fire. Please go to hell."

She wrote back: "You really must not write with your heart on fire. It's not literature. I really mean it." I did not reply. I am never going to write to her again.

I OWE her £50. I can only pay it back next year, Feb. or March, when my book comes out. Can I arrange payment through you, please? I hate her. She's a killer and very mean. She's written me mean, stinking letters for two years. I pretended not to notice. I'll pay back her money as soon as I can.

Bessie

About K, please refer to letter I wrote you 6 months ago.

[31]

P.O. Box 207, Francistown
14 November 1968

Dear Randolph,

I have not read *Turbott Wolfe*, but I cannot help but agree with you that my mother in particular, in her soul, was a goddess.

My action in withdrawing Howard from school might seem a weakness to you but indeed it has been something so painful that for a few days I could hardly stand on my feet. There is more which I have seen in the child and tried to save. My explanation is like putting the cart before the horse. It is like this. A child will often behave to people in general the way his parent treats him. I began to notice that he would do to other children what I did to him at home, that is, he unconsciously puts his arm around the neck of a friend and speaks to him most tenderly. Do you think he can go on doing that if he is beaten for so petty a thing as being a coloured? I don't mind what they call me or my child but why beat him? After all he came out of my factory so I deserve the beating, not he.

Now, I don't see why there cannot be a world where a person puts his arm around the neck of his brother. I prefer it that way. I mean I prefer him to continue that way, even if it is only I in the world who believe in the brotherhood of man. I can't reserve all that training of six years and perhaps I made a mistake in my last letter to refer to my ideas as creating a mess. Because that is all I am holding on to now.

It is far harder for me to take on the child's teaching myself. It was much easier to let him go to school and only play at teaching at home, which was what I had to do. Now I have had to put drill and sweat into it. I know mean humanity around here is rubbing their hands with glee. I have never known people being anything but horrible and enjoying the mental torture of another. The truth is that this mental torture will have to lead me to some conclusion more powerful than I have now. I have always hated soppy, wishy-washy love and truth, all the shit and crap but it is first one's mind that has to be sharpened up. You can only do so by putting it into fire. All this while I have asked for help which was never forthcoming. I don't care to appeal to the humanity in man any more. The more bastards leave me alone the more I shall come closer to the more profound causes for human suffering. Please don't think there is any weakness in me, Randolph. People with really weak characters cause an immense amount of suffering in the world. They destroy whole civilisations.

For all the apparent ambivalence of politics in Botswana and the deportation of refugees, Seretse is really a towering personality here. He is equally loved and hated. Everything else, like the colour of his children takes second place to his personality. Someone once told me in Serowe that he swore very badly when someone referred to his children as being coloured. In this respect he showed a typical African reaction. They don't like coloureds, for the simple reason that coloured people will often refer to African people as being stupid, though the bloody bastards have little education or social standing themselves while African people have very much more and an intense sense of social responsibility and cohesiveness. I know about the triumphant cohesiveness from having loved an African man. You can nearly get killed. The story travels from place to place along an unseen grape-vine and you are tightly surrounded by a net-work of spies. Your every move and word is closely watched and reported. People are deadly faithful to their own, not to you, the outsiders. One of the most painful moments of my life came when a Batswana woman said to me, with actual hatred: "What do you want running after the Batswanas?" No one acknowledged the fact that the man looked at me first. I would never have noticed him. But the humiliation of being run into the ground by these clever people is something I will never forget. Ever since then I have looked on an African man with real terror.

God, Randolph, the world must be much more simple than racialism or tribalism makes it. Or for that matter communism or capitalism. You know, I just feel sorry for everyone. To tell the truth I don't sit around thinking about the colour of my skin. I am taking a correspondence course in agriculture just right now. Plants are actually a very superior form of life. They are economically viable. They are the only form of life which manufactures its own food, in its own factory in a silent, self-absorbed way. I am just studying a thunderous description of this whole process, and it is the self-absorbed habits of plant life which so touch and fascinate my heart. No care about anything, just this inner concentration on creating energy and releasing it.

I am enclosing a part of the work my son is doing. Just right now I am drilling him into setting down his material in an ordered form. Once he grasps this I shall make his work more complicated. Also the other day he turned up with a very striking drawing of a mama and papa. I enclose it. Note that the mama and papa are gigantic and walk in a very stylish manner. The expressions on the tiny faces of the monstrous mama and papa are very interesting. The mama in particular looks a quite "come hither" girl. The papa has got his tongue in his cheek.

I am through with K and I know she is through with me. What she can't face is my last letter to her. She has never faced the truth about herself. She once wrote to me: I don't want human relationships to get a big thing. That is because she can't make space for others besides herself. There's no such thing as a bit-bit love and friendship. It is always going the whole hog of the way, even though you get hurt. I'm not that important to her. She only did not like my last letter. Other times I deliberately discussed the history of the Jews and God to avoid telling her off. I've run dry now on both subjects as far as my correspondence with her is concerned.

Heigh, ho, my friend. Writing to you puts me in a good mood. You are my best friend. You are practical, sane, and down to earth. The sanity I like most. The practical will change the world at the right time. Next to God you are my favourite person. Don't be upset if I quarrel with everyone. I enjoy raising hell. If there is no hell to raise I get out of style. Most times it is I who take the most blows and learn the deepest lessons.

As ever, Bessie

[32]

P.O. Box 207, Francistown
1 December 1968

Dear Randolph,

I received the books (short stories) you wanted reviewed. Enclosed is the work. I hope it is alright. I particularly liked *The Wedding of Zein* by the Arab writer. He is very good. Zein, the lead character is so original and vivid. I found it difficult to sum him up. And he is beautifully balanced out by the villagers. The whole book of the Arab writer is a TREASURE. Also the Nigerian proverbs. Did not like *Potent Ash* and said so.

Sincerely,
Bessie

[33]

P.O. Box 207, Francistown
14 January 1969

Dear Randolph,

Thank you for your letter of 27th Dec. I enjoyed the description of the English country-side very much. In fact I spent part of my childhood in an English mission orphanage in Natal, read all things English so England as a country is very familiar to me as a mental picture. You can't as a writer in Africa go in for such delicate, detailed descriptions of landscape the way English writers used to. The land is too vast and monumental. The power of the carvings of ancient Egyptian civilisation come nearest to an expression of Africa.

Up till now I have not seen any snow. It will be a miraculous sight for me, if I could travel one day. I also like all kinds of food, particularly Asian food. I keep these dreams in one part of my head.

I phoned Pat van Rensburg. I told him my son had not been at school since September. I find it embarrassing to explain ... especially to Pat. He helped me out of several scraps I got into here and now he will simply think this is my own invention. Also I have suffered such torture of mind that I do not like to refer to the matter. When I spoke to Pat he simply said that he would take Howard in at his primary school which is attached to Swaneng. As yet I do not know how to arrange this. I shall have to transfer myself to Serowe, the village from which I was chased. I have to release myself from the refugee conditions. I have to find accommodation which is almost non-existent in Botswana. But most important of all I want the child at Swaneng. I explained to Pat that I was taking a correspondence course in Tropical Agriculture with reference to food problems in developing countries. I would like to join his farmer's brigade. He said he did not think I could but he would make enquiries from the people who were running the brigade.

The reason why I phoned Pat is that I can't change myself ... from being a bushman, half-breed or what have you into anything to please anybody. I look like a Bushman, who is a despised tribe here. ... I am short in height. There is no one who is going to un-bushman me. All right. But few people know my heart and my mind. It travels all over the universe, like the wind. I really live with my heart and my mind, not my looks. Even if someone had to love me, it would surely be infantile of him to love my looks. He might love my heart or my mind.

You know who is the spreader of racialism? It is women,

71

always women. They are the real poison. Men can't afford to be racialists. They sleep around too much. Batswana men here sleep with Bushman women. I would query that as a man. You can't go kissing someone and then despise them for being a low nation. You have to touch that woman, then how can you go on preaching racialism? Still I hate everybody by now. I hate this stupidity.

If there were no love making in the world, racialism and prejudice would never die. It is the only way to break down insanity. You lose a part of yourself when you hold someone to you or they invade your isolation. After a time you don't notice how different they look from you. I never much liked white men but if I were married to one, I should defend him to the death because he would have become my own self. You can't hate your own mouth, can you? The man no longer has a mouth of his own. It is yours. The same with the hands, eyes, hair, nose and feet. I would apply this to a casual relationship as well as to a deeper, more emotional tie. I have seen love like this in my mind's eye and also observed the behaviour of a white woman married to a black man and vice versa. They don't look different. The woman looks, almost placidly, a part of the black man.

You might query why I say I never liked white men. He, a white man, carries with him all those things which have caused tremendous suffering to others, in the way he walks and talks to you. That there is no space in his heart to allow others to live on this earth, because they look different. There is something else. He is nervous, always irritable and lacks courage. From all these observations, I of course, exclude you but I am just saying that he may die as a species. Imagine going to bed with someone who is always irritable and demanding and petulant with many more nervous qualities. (I call all this jiggling). It can make a woman a complete nervous wreck.

Mind you, a black man lacks courage as far as his tribe is concerned, and his women. God, the genuine African woman is a dominating terror. I'm scared shitless myself, how much more must a man be? Otherwise, few African men jiggle. They stay in their own skin. They stand in their own skin like the rock of ages. Everyone who hates them for their looks will only wear themselves down and out of existence. There is nothing more solid, steady and eternal like the black man. I was observing all these qualities in my son. He picked them up from this environment. Nothing shakes him. But he will have a little more — total freedom from any prejudice.

Ha, you are so proud of all the writers who say they've been in the *New African*. Of course I have two publishers. Gollancz is the one who is more African orientated. When I filled in a publicity form for Gollancz I said: "Stories have been published in the N.A ..." The other thing was that Gollancz asked who could handle some publicity for the book and I sent them your name and address so that they could send you some of the advance copies. My book comes out with them in May. They have just sent me their catalogue of spring books and the title of my book is there with a picture and a little information about me. The picture looks quite pretty, mind you.

No, I do not agree with Lord Jim. I take the view that the longer you live the more you absorb and learn. You reach a stage of total wisdom for your age and time. To me, boldness and wisdom are spiritual qualities and the spirit is like wine or a flower. Its growth and unfoldment is slow and gradual until a state of perfection is reached. The process is also subconscious or hidden but very determined. I know some people do not unfold in this way but I accept it as a principle which could be applied to all mankind. The truth is, those who show this totality of wisdom and perfection in their maturity, like a Jesus or Buddha, actually made more than superhuman efforts to achieve it. And once achieved they never let up. To keep at a certain peak demands a total concentration of effort. The thing is, you get born to it. There are factors in your destiny which make you endure such suffering as would kill a normal human physique. Generally applied, many, many people have been through this. By the time you come to the end of *Dr Zhivago*, you wonder how any human being could have endured so much suffering, for the end chapters of the book nearly crack you mentally. It was more terrible there because the darkness was so total, the evil so vicious and stupid, the loss that much more great. That woman, Lara, with her terrible cry: "Oh Yurochka, so here we are again. The way God brings us together. How terrible, think of it! Oh, I can't bear it! Oh Lord! I cry and cry! Think of it! Again something just our kind, just up our street. Your going, that's the end of me. Again something big, inescapable. The riddle of life, the riddle of death, the beauty of genius, the beauty of loving — that, yes, that we understood. As for such petty trifles as re-shaping the world — these things, no thank you, they are not for us ..."

There is so much more in those last words of that woman. "My heart has no peace. I cannot live for pity and misery. But you see, I haven't taken to drink as so many people do. A drunken woman, that would be the end of everything ..."

The crux of it is: Again something big, inescapable. It is only those who are of the Gods and have been since eternity who look loss steadily in the face knowing it is inescapable because the process of suffering creates something big. Pasternak grasped the stuff of which spiritual giants are made and what applies to him applies to every spiritual giant. He was talking about giants of the soul, not the petty

74

torturers and how they would shape the future. He could afford to end the book ..."To the two ageing friends sitting by the window it seemed that this freedom of the spirit was there (already), that on that very evening the future had become tangible ... They felt a peaceful joy for this holy city (Moscow), and for the whole land and for the survivors and their children ..."

The land was made holy by people's suffering. Subconsciously, the same process is going on in South Africa. That land is being made holy by all the tears of the black man which have dropped on to the soil. They made giants of ordinary people and one day, quite soon, the unfoldment will be reached. I make a parallel of it all in my own life because I can feel this process of unfoldment and growth. There was always the glimmer of happiness and it was snatched away before you could stretch out your hand. There was no resting place but a boomerang action from one disaster to another. After a time you rested in the disaster itself and looked on the total wreckage of your life with something that resembles holding on. But it is a threadbare existence, so horrible and bleak.

It would be more horrible to me had there not been a God at the centre of it, much more clear and vivid than Pasternak could picture. You begin to see very clearly the logic in the statement: "He will pull down the mighty from their seats and exalt those of low degree. He will fill the hungry with good things and the rich he will send empty away ..." The fulfilment of this vision will be carried out by men and women who have the souls of giants. And quite soon too. You may not see your place in this because you feel ordinary and humble and I know that. But how are the mighty to be pulled down from their seats except by the ordinary and humble people? The whole world has had enough of the

75

bloody bastards who can only rule by preventative detention, blood, greed, caste, class, spies and the secret service.
They look towards the day when everyone will be free, with
a right to live on this earth even though they look ugly with
a green nose and roughly-cast features. People who have a
sentiment about children surprise me. Those children grow
up into adults, sometimes with ugly looks and flat noses.
The love must be total, all the way. How I hate sentimental
bastards. They are so cruel. They slobber over helpless
things but they hate the totality of life. Life is everything
but mostly it is your eyes and your heart you are killing
when you kill your brother.

Much of my present state of mind, Randolph, is due to
much suffering. I learnt to look beyond all illusions and delusions to that which is real. There is nothing left now but a
love which includes others as my own self. I first have to say:
That is my mouth. That is my hair. That is mine. Then I
can't hate or destroy that which is mine. It is something
deeper than the brotherhood of man. It is the oneness of the
soul with all living things, whether human or animal or vegetable. It means that I would say you are my own self,
whether you think differently or not or have any objections
to my laying claim to your hair or eyes or what. It is a reality
because I have experienced it as such. It makes me struggle
to find a new definition of love and harmony. It also makes
me want to laugh because finally I am the ocean in which all
things live and move and have their being and for them to
think they are separate and apart from my life is not possible.

D. H. Lawrence achieved this vision. I did not understand
what he was saying but when you reach it — this unity of
soul with life, you say: "All things changed. The blossoms of
the universe turned and looked another way."

Bessie

76

2 FRANCISTOWN: 15 January 1966 – 14 January 1969

When Rain Clouds Gather was a long time coming, but Bessie wrote more calmly and cheerfully in the two years it took. The correspondence with many who wrote to her after "The Woman from America" tailed off, but I know of only one major set-to, with a serious-minded woman, K in the letters, who never appeared to me the monster Bessie was to depict her after the first careless rapture. She is recalled as Camilla in *A Question of Power*. I know of no lasting pen-friendships from that date.

I heard from Machin that Simon and Schuster had accepted the book and wrote at once to Bessie. She commiserated very kindly about my great friend, the radical Liberal leader Patrick Duncan, whom we had both known in Cape Town and who died of aplastic anaemia in London in 1967 [26]. We shared disgust and disappointment at the corruption of so many of the Pan-Africanist Congress leaders in exile. Her story "The Coming of the Christ Child," which did not appear until long after, was, of course, the testament of her veneration for its founding President, Robert Mangaliso Sobukwe [106]. She became more secure in Botswana, her bitter reproaches turned to expressions of love for the country and its people. She could now see Patrick van Rensburg and Swaneng Hill in a proper light, and the admission of Howard to Swaneng, though it meant a difficult return to Serowe, with all its painful associations, was a moment of happiness. She began to mention things we had not yet shared, like the tragedy of her parentage — her white mother's insanity and her unknown African father. I quoted Plomer's lines about Mabel, the white woman who married Zachary Msomi, near the end of *Turbott Wolfe* (1925) [31]:

> As she emerged across the open sward (dew-drenched and sunlit) her departure acquired a colossal valedictory significance ... and she became the goddess of the future, going out to suffer. What was her name? Her name was Eurafrica.

77

The New African remained a bond. We had published some belligerent, pre-black-consciousness free verse called "Things I don't Like" in July 1962 and many stories and reviews since, but she had not until now spoken in favour of the magazine. The words in our fiftieth issue, which she said I had "pinched" [27] (from her 11 December 1967 letter), were both in praise of the magazine and a comment on Stokely Carmichael's appeal, in our July 1967 issue. Carmichael had asked for support for the Students Non-violent Co-ordinating Conference as "a national power base of gathered strength, a new political apparatus." In 1968 we published "God and the Underdog: Thoughts on the Rise of Africa," a powerful piece in which she juxtaposed conversations with two British volunteers. To one she said:

"There is nothing that moves me more deeply than the history of the Jews. They of all people have experienced most deeply and profoundly that God is the real Owner of the Universe." Being caught up in this thought, I was quite taken aback when the volunteer turned on me irritably and said: "I don't like the way you say God is the Owner of the Universe." The first thing that occurred to me after this was only to walk away as quickly a possible. Because I was enraged. Because I wanted to say something like this: "Do you think your bloody motor-car is the Owner of the Universe? Do you think a pip-squeak little jiggling white man like you is God? Why, you could drop dead this very minute."

The other, "in the hut of an old Batswana man", was with a Cambridge graduate, to whom the old man said:

"I think the Good God does not like all the bad things in the world." This had a profoundly moving effect on the Cambridge graduate. He even absent-mindedly drank a cup of tea into which several flies had fallen. It was really this volunteer, who was so deeply moved by a vision of God through an old Batswana man, that, for some time, made me extremely enthusiastic about voluntary help, quite out of touch with reality. It's there. Some of it is good. But Africa is going to rise to a great height of civilisation, and this is going to be done, in the last resort, by African brains, and by God, who, Bessie explains, must, to her, be female and black.

In January 1969, *When Rain Clouds Gather* at last appeared and her cup was nearly full, but for the silence of one of her magazine editors and the imprisonment of another, the Ugandan Rajat Neogy, of *Transition*. What was it that I quoted from *Lord Jim* that set her off on those final pages? Such resilience, after the deep woe of her self-identification with the San (Bushmen), or Masarwa as the Batswana call them. I ended my reply (the first of my letters in the Bessie Head Archive in Serowe.) "Don't go crazy with excitement," I soothed, "though I'm sure the book [not yet published in Britain] merits it."

3. Francistown – Serowe
15 January 1969 – 16 January 1971

[34]

P.O. Box 207, Francistown
15 January 1969

Dear Randolph,

Just as I was posting my letter to you I also received the first advance copy of my book from Simon & Schuster. Publication date with them is 11th March, 1969.

They wanted me to take some books for advance publicity but from where I am I can't handle this. The idea is to send it to influential people who will spread the word around. The day I know such people will indeed be the day! I really want it to get to black people because it is for them, say that Negro people one day swoop over here. I'd like that public. Do you know if John Clarke is still around? I can't get a letter out of him. He's the editor of *Freedomways* and also I hear that Neogy is in jail. Can I leave everything to you? I asked S & S to send you one copy first and then you could let them know how many you could handle for advance publicity.

Seemingly quite by accident S & S designed the cover of the book in the colours of the Botswana flag. There's my nearly pitch black face, hair and eyebrows in a huge photograph on the cover framed by blue and white stripes. The flag — blue, black and white. Think the old cronies here would appreciate that? I not only write about development, I get the goddam flag too.

My everlasting friend, forgive the vanity. But let me know as soon as possible what you think about the book. Don't get excited and dash off one of those illegible letters I can't decipher. Please sit down and type it. I want to keep it to read several times and I get so mad when I can't read your handwriting.

God, God, God but it looks terrific. I feel this way because it is only a first baby. I am going out of my mind. I am going out of my head.

Now please write to me as quickly as possible.

Bessie

[35]

Poste Restante, Serowe
29 January 1969

Dear Randolph,

Please note NEW ADDRESS, Poste Restante, Serowe. Taking Howard to school to-morrow. On arrival here found new post office was about to be built, thus no box numbers yet.

Should you have already written letter will be transferred to above address.

Suffering from joyous mental confusion over book.

Also God only knows how the move went so smoothly. Also big number of refugees being airlifted this week to Zambia for studies. Much feels good. Howard has new pair of shoes for school. I am mixed up.

Bessie

P.S. Don't forget to note change of address.

[36]

Dear Randolph,

Thanks for your letter of the 9th. I received the clipping
and also preserved your scrawl across the newspaper which I
loved very much. See here, my friend, I absent-mindedly
might have put myself in quite a shit with Gollancz. They
wrote saying their solicitor was worried about a line in the
book: "The Chiefs all had syphilis ..." Not thinking very
deeply, I wrote back saying: "Don't worry, a lot of people in
Africa have VD". They might either laugh or be very repelled
by that thoughtless statement. The thing is a doctor said it.
He said he had never seen so much VD as in Botswana, with
side complications and horrors and he was a black man. I was
thinking about the doctor and not the effect on Gollancz. I
am always telling people to shit their pants and this time it is
me. Once the letter was posted I began to sweat and thought:
"God, now why did I write that?"

The truth is, my everlasting friend I might have done it
out of hatred for the hangdogs of this village. They are fuming that I am back. First, I am on a refugee list here still. I
shall be getting money from UN in March. I had the left-
over pieces of a refugee allowance. So I sat down and contin-
ued with my studies. I am being given money by UN for a
course I'm taking in Tropical Agriculture. The fact that I am
sitting at home and still buying food so worked up the
lunatics of this village. They say I am getting money from a
man who visits me in the night time though I wonder if they
can produce the man. This is alright by me because not one
of them is ever going to see my sex organs. But the gossip

works like this: I walked into a shop and asked for a half pound of cheese. The crazy Motswana behind the counter said to me: "Look here, if you don't treat us with respect, we can't serve you."

What has that got to do with asking for a half pound of cheese in a normal voice? First of all I walked out of the shop thinking I must have gone mad. I could not believe my ears, till I heard the story about the man who visits me at night time and gives me money.

I can't really take this, my friend. I have lived for some time in a state of permanent nervous breakdown. Howard is at school. It was Swaneng I came here for, not to be killed by lunatics. I doubt I will survive. There is not one sane person in this village. I can't go to Pat's place, though I would like to. I am still shaking at the thought that Howard has a school. I am so worked up about this that I don't want anything to go wrong and perhaps Pat does not like me because I am always in a mess. If I went to sit and study at Swaneng during the day, something is sure to go wrong somewhere. I can't believe now that I can live except for hours and hours on my own but my mind is distracted with intense dislike for the people of this country. I am beginning to really loathe them. I might like your offer of a visit to England, sometime but how to leave here? How?

This might also seem strange. I am on the point of being a little rich from that best-seller I have there (ha, ha) but by next week, or so I shall be destitute. I thought about the four pounds four shillings you offered me for the reviews and I wanted to ask if you could send it to me urgently in British postal orders, please. It will keep me going until about March 10th when my allowance from UN will arrive.

Goldblatt's pictures make me look like Kwame Nkrumah, full of strain and stress in the face. The one on the dust jacket is not so bad but I have seen another where I looked like Nkrumah. I hope the one he gave you has a normal expression. I am not photogenic, though in some of my other incarnations I used to be. This thought of the other prettier incarnations makes me very shy of having my face published ...

Much love. Don't be absent-minded about the four pounds. I can't open an account or explain to the shop keepers that although I am not working I have a best-seller. They won't give me food.

Bess

P.S. If you get pally with Sarah Hayes explain casually that the VD was a light-hearted joke.

[37]

Poste Restante, Serowe
2 May 1969

Dear Randolph,

I knew you would do it! It has taken me almost three hours to decipher your scrawled note of 27th April. I am still not sure if I have made out every word.

In many ways you must be more than my blood brother because you always pick the crux of the matter — the people with no shoes — and it is more meaningful to me than you would believe, as though your note completed a cycle in my mind that began some three years ago. I had made mention in the book of the no shoes because of a very vivid dream I had three years ago. I dreamt I was sitting on a bed in a big house and a group of such people of Africa walked into the room. They lay down at the foot of the bed and each one placed a foot on the bed. Their feet were cut and bleeding and they were all very poor. The intent was to show me the feet of poverty. Out of the group an old woman stood up. She had a dirty white purse in her hand out of which she took a soiled five pound note and held it towards me. She said: "You have to buy three things" and mentioned them. She handed me the five pounds. Someone sitting near me on the bed handed her a ten pound note, brand new. This is the cause of the strange economics in my book, whereby you spend five pounds and get ten pounds back as change. You could say that the visionary force of that dream carried me through *Rain Clouds* because I wrote it under such pressure and speed that I was half unaware of what I was doing.

It is painful to me that what I built up and suffered for and dreamt about has left me with very little dreams and visions at present. Perhaps *Rain Clouds* was all in vain for there is such a black, bitter and violent rage in my heart. I sometimes can't look at the face of a black man or woman without at the same time thinking that they are the epitome of all that is grasping, greedy, cruel, back stabbing and a betrayal of all that is good in mankind. Half of this was that I had to be admitted to hospital with a nervous breakdown. Half of it was this village. I came here because of the school. It is still the school that keeps me here but I really live on some swinging pendulum with a very precarious mental balance.

A dream or a vision may be ahead of events and this is what I suffer from because I know what can happen and how perfect the world can become. Sometimes I have seen people have a change of heart but the process is a shattering one. There is someone who does the changing, by force, and the changer of hearts gets a nervous breakdown. There is very little to buoy me up at present. Not long after I came out of hospital I received one of your scrawled notes with a cutting from the London *Bookseller*. It said: "Bessie Head, the ebullient Botswanan ..." If only they knew. Here I am Bessie Head, the

Bushman dog … Where can I go because there is no home for me anywhere and I have become blind and deaf to any such thing as human kindness or affection, as though I reached a precipice and just jumped over and nothing reached me anymore.

You are right. *Rain Clouds* was meant for the people with no shoes. But something has died in me, Randolph. I cannot endure the sight and face of a black man or woman any longer. It is as though I want to scream and scream and scream and scream every day or just walk out and kill the first person I see, stone dead. I thought of every way to leave this hateful village of spite, cruelty, gossip and insanity but I'd only get to the border again and have no way of leaving this country. You can't even say: God help me because often that is just a mockery and maybe God is just as evil and malicious as these people and long planned my destruction. Only he was waiting until I was finally broken, like now.

Bessie

[38]

Poste Restante, Serowe
24 May 1969

Dear Randolph,

I am very relieved to hear from you. Not long after posting my last letter to you, I had two strange dreams which have troubled me.

Dream No. 1: There was this bright sunlit courtyard with some white people sitting about. They looked like the type who work at Swaneng. I kept on hearing someone crying, in a terrible voice. Being distressed I ran about looking for the person who was crying. Not finding "it," I approached a woman and asked: "Who is crying?" She kept her face reserved and compressed her mouth as though she did not like me ... I awoke in a sweat of terror.

Dream No. 2: (This happened the following night.) This time it is a group of black people having a discussion. One said, referring to me: "There was no one harming her this time. She just blew up for nothing." So someone else said: "Are you sure she doesn't need treatment?" So the first voice said: "No there's nothing wrong with her. She could do with a bit of vaseline on the behind." So the second voice said: "Alright, put on the vaseline, and throw her out of the window."

I again awoke in a sweat of terror.

It was dream number one which was particularly disturbing. Since I could not see who was crying, on awaking, I assumed it must be God who did not like being referred to as evil and malicious and that on receipt of my letter you must have had a discussion with him and complained. I must say I am very sorry for that part of the letter and in case you are managing some of the affairs of God I hope you will put matters right for me. You may note that the people of Dream number two appear ashamed of themselves being well aware that they have caused me trouble. The whole business of ending up in hospital went like this:

Since the day I arrived here I kept on hearing people snickering as I walked down the road. Several approached me to ask what I had done to the child I gave birth to in Francistown. Then an old woman said she was hungry with no food in the house. Unthinkingly I gave her ten shillings. It must have been this old hag who was placed to spread the rumour because after that I was insulted by stupid, illiterate servers in a shop, on the grounds that I am receiving money from someone who visits me in the night time. This makes me too low to be served as a customer. (I mentioned this bit to you concerning the request for a half a pound of cheese.)

87

The thing is, people know I was chased from this village under strange circumstances. They also know it involved a gentleman who was forced into marriage and who protested. They also know that a lot of influential people don't like me and how dare I set foot back here. What really made me mad is that they created for me a reputation so horrible. How can I be like the run-of-the-mill woman here who is a prostitute and thinks nothing of throwing a baby down a pit toilet? Such things are so far removed from my own life. Only now and then a bit of gossip reaches me about what people do and still it never really enters my mind because I don't know the people concerned and it is usually brought to me (at least in Francistown) by a casual male friend who drops in for a cup of tea.

The thing is they really believed it, those things they confronted me with. Eventually I cornered three of the buggers in a room and started screaming: "You bloody bastards." They had to call the police, who at first wanted to take me to jail but since I was shaking from head to foot they took me to hospital instead.

Strangely enough it relieved my heart to say all these things I did say in that last letter. I thought them for a long time but said nothing. Once I said I hate the black man, it just passed from my mind the same as it is difficult, after writing all those blood curdling items on the white man to remember what it is I hate him for. It gets lost once you spit it out.

Bessie

[39]

Dear Randolph,

I can't apologise for inflicting my troubles on you. If I can't depend on you, then who must I turn to? I am afraid you will have to put up with the idea of being my imaginary father because I can think of no one else suited to the job. There is no one who can decide what kind of children they ought to have and you can grumble as much as you like but you are burdened with me for the purposes of destiny.

Things are alright these days and life goes on an even keel. I must have been ill for all those three months Howard had no school only I could not afford to admit it then. There were things here in this village, though, that were pretty funny. Since many women trade themselves, I have not yet heard them complaining about being insulted by illiterate shopkeepers. Men don't usually insult prostitutes because they visit them at night, nor do people snicker when they walk down the road as they did to me. I thought it was a concerted effort by the village to oust me. It went on for some time but seems to have died down now, the snickering and insults. Only I am uneasy in my mind. Perhaps I did not realise how much, what is known as a mixed breed, is really deeply hated by African people. The hate is more active than what it is possible to direct towards the white man because a half caste has less defence, dignity or property. It can't work out that straight for the future where the white man drops down and then you oust all the half breeds or mass slaughter them. For one thing, Pat's people are a spoke in the wheels. There are just too many good white women marrying

89

African men and their children are not going to be milksops. The other thing is, I put the matter to a simple test in my own life, though I say the love is in the past tense, I did take that certain gentleman I got chased away from here for, as my own property. One day I approached the gentleman and said: "I have never seen anyone with such an ugly face like you, with a squat, ugly African nose." Mind you, he was highly pleased by the remark. Could I have said that to anyone else who was not my property without getting beaten for being a coloured? Or racialist? There is no one else whom I can say is ugly without the person getting violently annoyed, especially if I picked on a certain facial feature. Indeed the gentleman has a remarkably ugly nose such as most African people do not have, like it was just roughly plastered on his face.

I am really uncertain of my future. It was mostly for Howard's sake that I came back this way. There is nothing for me here and I am a highly dubious commodity to Pat Van Rensburg. He's seen me too often dragged to the police station in a screaming rage. People only get to know about that, not those long, endless, lonely hours of silent contemplation where months and months pass by without me saying a word to anyone except Howard and writing. These people surely did not believe their prostitute and baby killer reputation that they built up for me. I am unapproachable by any man. They are petrified by the rush of words as though it makes them impotent. Also I have a fearful aversion for men unless they are of good character. I nearly killed Harold and I could not endure such an experience again.

I did not like the reviews from either England nor America, except one that appeared in the *Illustrated London News* by someone called Dominic Le Foe. They all misread the book, each according to his own particular prejudice. What I said about God in the book was related very closely with Makhaya's inner struggles. I simply want God in mankind instead of up in the sky. Put him inside a man and a man is obliged to live a noble life, where other people can depend on him to be truthful in his dealings. People brought up on Christianity think God has nothing to do with them. He is someone who turns water into wine. They just go on shitting up the world and feel no responsibility for their character or anything they do. It was put so simply and yet supposedly intelligent people could not recognise that. They thought I was at the white man. I don't give a damn about the fools. I was pulling either myself up or Africa. I have just heard that the book is under embargo by the SA govt.

Bessie

P.S. Send me the reviews by Caroline and Myrna. Also two copies of the *New African* review.

[40]

Poste Restante, Serowe
11 June 1969

Dear Randolph,

I am forced to write a supplementary letter as I forgot a few things. The publishing house which produced the book of short stories by the Kibera and Kahiga brothers, which I slashed in *The New African*, also run a magazine. They obtained my address somewhere and sent me a two-paged review of the same trashy book, with no comment. The reviewer went to great length to describe the tension of line and economic prose of the two immature writers. People produce that kind of literature in Standard six and here was a reviewer going over the silly stories, which had nothing in them, line by line. There was nothing to lift the heart or stimulate the mind and I just don't know what they mean by tension of the lines, when the writers are still babies. I had to sweat over the book because I promised you the review but it gave me a terrible pain in the head.

Another thing. God knows I am impulsive. For one thing I hate anyone to feel left out but I am chewing my teeth in agony at the type of literature in the *New African* produced by the Black Power movement in America. Each time I get the *New African* I try to grind my way through the articles of S.E. Anderson but I give up half way. God it is a boring dead end. What the hell does he mean by the apolitical struggle of the masses? Is the goddam bugger not a mess too or is he some divine creature above us who has been special-ly born to lead the black man to the promised land? I could kill myself for what I said about Martin Luther King because I don't only prefer the speeches he made, I can see his promised land now. At the time I was suffering, not knowing where it would all end and I was just about to contemplate violence. Not so now. I accept what King said that the black man can't afford to do to the white man what the white man did to him. Look at the music in this ... "There once lived a people, a great people" ... so said King of the black man. I have been suffering for that letter I wrote to you, where I seemed to be impatient with King. I feel I have grasped him but I am one jump ahead. I really see the promised land very vividly, only not for the black man alone but for all people alive on the earth.

There is something deadly wrong with the thought of the black power people. It has no heart. Its apparently compli-cated intellectual reasoning is derived from the inferiority complex which wants to impress perhaps "whitey" that the black man has got brains. It is all sham and pose and ego and

92

something I can't stomach. I am sorry for this late conclusion but still in my heart I always feel that every crank ought to have his say. I was thinking deeply about the Black Power people because I have six L.P.s of Miriam Makeba, who is married to Stokeley Carmichael. I cannot help loving the woman's music. She can put over anything, even the huffing, panting noises of primitive tribal people. Her style is simple too. Her love songs are the nearest I have ever come to the most heavenly music... those weaving, difficult rhythms, and all the flowers and birds and sunsets. That is life. Surely in heaven the black man knows such things exist? I feel those things in King's speeches. I want to tell you about Miriam Makeba. Once when I was working for *Drum* publications, they sent me to interview her after the *King Kong* show. A reporter friend who knew her arranged for us to have lunch together. When I greeted her, she did not reply. She just stared back at me with still, black eyes. I said a few more words, and then shut up because I could see the woman hated me although it was the first time we met. When I walked back to work I said to the reporter friend: "What gives with that woman?" So he said: "She doesn't like coloureds."

There is a vague story in my mind. The woman's first love was apparently a coloured man from who she had a child. The family said: "Voetsak, get away Kaffir." I wonder why I have to find all these things out? Because I have never belonged there and to go through all kinds of hell makes me so mad and get hated for what I could not do, drives me round the bend. When I thought back on that interview with Miriam it cost me an effort to like her music. Then the feeling wore away. I would have lost a lot. That's half the reason why I don't like anyone shut up or turned down.

Bessie

[41]

Poste Restante, Serowe
23 July 1969

Dear Randolph,

Certain adults, including myself, are as excited as the children here about the moon. Howard put his artistic ability to work and I enclose one of the masterpieces, he drew on my cigarette box. Voice of America is a disgusting radio station, but I have to agree with them that Russia would not have let the whole world in on such a party. Due to behaving like the children I tuned into Voice of America for the continuous broadcasts. They said: "We are now on our African programme." (Then the announcer said: 'Here's the news in special English.' He switched to the tone of a school teacher talking to four year olds — NOW ARE YOU LISTENING *CAREFULLY* LITTLE BOY!) It soured matters for me. Here in Africa we hear the news in ordinary English. No African announcer talks like that to illiterate people. In fact, you will get some of the most alert, original, crisply-spoken English on this continent, whether a man is educated or not. It got me to wondering if their propaganda was deliberately evil or just plain stupid. I can't credit those Americans with such brains, because it really takes brains to be evil.

Well, I have been working on some ideas which as you say, must cut right through racial appearance to link man to man. What I enclose is still tentative. The parts I marked with red pencil, are really very vivid inner perceptions. The process by which I can make such a claim is not really as simple as I say there. What it really means is that such people are really a chosen few and they have (or their souls have) been involved in goodness for centuries. I have to out-

line this vision more vividly and impressively and I feel it is
the language of the future. I had written it for one of my editors in America who is also a friend, but I had you in mind
when I wrote it.

Sincerely,
Bessie

[42]

Bessie Head
18 August 1969

Dear Randolph,

I was unable to get a British postal order from the Post
Office here for the £25 for K. I shall have to go to the bank.
Postal orders cancelled since, I think, devaluation.

Bessie

[43]

Poste Restante, Serowe
22 August 1969

Dear Randolph,

How can you damage my eyesight like this? To say I can't
read your handwriting is an understatement!

There is a shocking story behind Sammy Peterson's recent
deportation from Botswana. I heard it yesterday from our
refugee welfare officer, Mr Terence Finley.

Sammy is the first such case since the Refugee Recognition
& Control bill came out more than a year ago. We go through
a rigmarole like this: We are all detained in jail for a few
hours then handed a form with any number of restrictions

but the main thing is that it is no longer a matter of just deporting people and no one has been since this rigmarole started.

Now, Sammy came, for the second time, and was secretly concealed in the home of a refugee for about two or three weeks. The refugee then became afraid and reported the matter to Terence Finley. Finley said: 'Come on, let's get this thing above board,' and he took Sammy Peterson to the police, who immediately placed him in detention. Terence Finley then raced to Gaborone and got an interview with a certain Mr Heady who works in the office of the President. This Mr Heady said he would look into the Sammy Peterson case. Mr Finley also promised to get Peterson to London.

When Mr Finley came back to Francistown he found that a security official, named Sherrit, had already deported Sammy Peterson back to South Africa. Finley said: "But why did you do that when I am here to help get the man out of the country?"

Sherrit said: "I could not take the risk of keeping the man here a day longer. He had a wild look in his eyes." He told Finley he had deported Peterson on his old order, without the knowledge of the authorities in Gaborone. Peterson was declared insane in South Africa. A Botswana doctor, Dr Moeti, declared him sane and issued a certificate of sanity. Dr Moeti is at the moment in London and is expected to give evidence on Sammy's behalf through Amnesty International who are making arrangements to have him taken out from South Africa. Sammy Peterson blew up a phone booth.

I have received word that about a thousand pounds will come my way soon. I want to pay back that damn K woman the fifty pounds I owe her. I say damn for all the hurt she gave me, not for the loan of money for which I was grateful. Please let me know if I could send you the fifty pounds by postal order, to repay her and if that is alright? I can't stand her getting her claws into me again. She is a malicious woman.

I have completed a short novel, half commissioned by Simon & Schuster. They promoted *Rain Clouds* as a book for kids. Then they asked for something like *Catcher in the Rye*, of 30,000 words. When I wrote back and said I don't write for a particular audience, they wrote back a nice letter, so I won't feel hurt. I sent them a sizzler, full of illegitimate children. I want to see if they mean what they say. It's a masterpiece, but certainly not for little children. They damn well went and advertised *Rain Clouds* for teenagers in spite of all I said about the sex organs. A young boy here, though, tells me, that he read Mickey Spillane at 13. He says boys at least, think about nothing else but Spillane's subjects all through adolescence.

Of course I am not complaining, as long as the book sells. But I don't like the tab — the writer for teenagers. Why can't they let me alone, just as a writer? This request from S & S came from the editor of the children's book dept.

Bessie

Athena School book series, London, have also bought *Rain Clouds*. I have 5 publishers!!

[44]

Poste Restante, Serowe
3 October 1969

Dear Randolph,

Yes please send me Prof. Mbiti's book on African religions and I shall review it for the N.A.

I am living in some kind of bedlam just now. Pat van

Rensburg gave me a small piece of ground just outside Swaneng school grounds and on it I am building a small house, with two rooms, and a thirdd divided into bathroom, toilet and kitchen. I am building it with the thousand pounds I received from the paperback sales of *Rain Clouds* to Bantam books. The house is minute but the pride is overwhelming. It is the first brick thing I shall ever own. The cause of the bedlam is that I keep on getting under the feet of the builders to see how the bricks go up. The house is being built for me by some young boys who are just about to graduate from Pat's project, the Serowe Builders Brigade. The house, when complete will cost me about six hundred to seven hundred pounds.

Tied to this is that Pat asked me to join a vegetable garden project with a group of villagers who live near the school. They are also starting a nursery for trees. The one thing that retards everything is that the vegetable garden does not seem to have a sound financial aim in mind. People are asked to contribute voluntary labour. The whole of Swaneng was built like that but somehow you can't do that with vegetables. I thought it had to be made financial from the start with all the capitalist tags even though it is to be done co-operatively. People who have no employment then, can make a living.

Though I talk like this I am having a terrible headache about the one thousand pounds I received from Bantam books. I have never had more than three hundred pounds in the bank, in the savings branch. With it goes a little book and you sign a paper to withdraw money. So the bank put my money into my savings book account. Then I had to place a deposit of three hundred and forty rand on my house. I went to the bank and they said I could not withdraw so much money. Then some one said I ought to open a chequing account with the bank. The thing is, I have never made out a cheque in my life and the thought so terrifies me that every time I think of buying a cheque book, I go cold from head to toe. I have been totally unable to pluck up the courage to get a cheque book. I say I will do it next week. Then next week. I don't know what appals me so much about writing out cheques.

Now you say at the top of your letter that I can send a cheque to you to repay the amount I owe K. Can I not send you the money in British postal orders? Is there difficulty in getting a British postal order accepted when it comes from this side? Who knows how long it will take me to open a cheque account. I can't manage it on my own and even thought of hanging myself first. I wonder what's wrong with me. It is just that I am faced with a totally new situation and my imagination undoes me. When you receive a cheque, there is such a bother to get it cashed. What happens when you write one out? That is where I close my eyes in agony.

Sincerely,
Bessie

[45]

Poste Restante, Serowe
18 October 1969

Dear Randolph,

As you will see from the enclosed postal order for K, my nervous system still prevents me from buying a cheque book. I laughed a lot about that poor Stephen man. Banks are places full of snobs. I wonder how people save money in Russia or what they have there.

The matter about the money I owe K goes like this:

First she sent me twenty-five pounds for the typewriter. In her letter she said: "You can pay it back in good time."

In a later letter she said: "Tell us what you may need and N and I may make a small contribution." The woman was such a complicated mixture of good and evil and child-like viciousness that I did not really know what I was communicating with. What I faced at the time was starvation. So, following the cheque for twenty-five pounds, I thought I'd accept the offer of help but as a small loan and I was getting so much encouragement from my American editors over *Rain Clouds* that I could foresee the day when I'd pay it all back. She therefore sent me some small cheques of five pounds. It did not go so high but I did not keep account of it. I just hazard that it amounted to another twenty-five pounds, but it could be more. Then she would say: "Here is five pounds for sweets for your little boy." So I am not so sure about the other amounts except that she has a record of them.

Therefore the other amount might be thirty pounds or forty pounds and not another twenty-five. I think I asked her to loan me twenty pounds at a desperate moment. So I thought I would first send her the twenty-five pounds for the type-writer which she asked me to pay back and see what she has to say about the rest of the money she sent me. Could you please send her this twenty-five pounds and tell her it is repayment for the type-writer. Ask her how much more I owe her. Please forgive me Randolph for this sordid matter but there is hell and hell and I am so broken down I cannot stand much more of it. I am very grateful for your assistance over this.

You are very rash to ask me what I would like for my new house. I wanted to give it a name, after the title of my book, not the whole title but only *Rain Clouds*. Now, if you can find a friend who can do it out of love, can you get the name made for me so that I can attach it to my house? I used to see these name plates in Cape Town. Tell him or her not to make it a fancy, expensive job and can it be done on material that would not be heavy for postage. The whole house is being erected entirely on the Bantam book paperback rights and it really calls for endless and wonderful conferences with the builders. Everything is geared to keeping costs down. I make payments piece-meal but they are always there on demand. The thing is, the house and the book go together and I would very much like to call the house *Rain Clouds*. I wanted the name done by someone who would do it out of affection. Indeed, there are some artistic types at Swaneng but I really have no friends there or anyone I could call for some gesture of affection.

I have also received Mbiti's book on African Religions and Philosophy. From the first few pages, he is my man. There have been people here who have appeared holy to me, within themselves and I am inclined myself to pick up God or goodness directly from life as people live it. It is the cause of the constant flux between bitterness and joy.

Pat asked me if I would organise the garden project. They have a garden going at Swaneng which supplies the hospital and a school with vegetables. I have been working in this garden for three weeks now, to duplicate the plan and methods of water conservation in the garden to be started by the villagers. I hope to mmove over to my new house in November.

Affectionately,
Bessie

[46]

Dear Randolph,

I had to hurry a little with this review as you said you wanted it urgently. I liked working on it up till today when a sudden ailment makes me feel very depressed. So I am not sure it is good enough. I have a fever and it makes me very irritable.

A lot that Mbiti says about people in Africa is confirmed by my own feelings. I did not touch on his chapters on witchcraft, initiation and such like because that is a rapidly dying world and really embarrassing to the young who are accommodating many new things. I also think ceremonies, witchery, etc are a form of snobbery to see where you fit in society. It is surely not important. I picked on those things which are a pointer to the future. Say, each nation prepares its own destiny.

Excuse me, I am feverish and incoherent. Let me know if you would like a re-do of the enclosed review. I rush to send it because you wanted it immediately but I am so sick I think it is not so good. We have been having terrible rain. I must have been bitten by a mosquito in the night which was carrying some plague.

Sincerely,
Bessie

P.S. I sent you a cheque for R50 for K. Let me know what the banks say there. You must not lose 5c or so helping me, so if they are going to charge you something on the cheque, let me know so that I can enclose 5c in the letter.

[47]

Dear Randolph,

I can just manage a scrawl but not illegible like your letter! I'm cleaning and settling in, in *Rain Clouds*. It is such a beautiful home, and I am since yesterday, when the final payments were made, the owner of the house, a tool shed and a small seedling nursery. I still owe Pat R300 for the plumbing as an extra as it is being installed by his plumber. I hope to clear this on some royalties or the sale of a short novel I completed about 2 months ago. This to the *New Yorker* — the piece asked for by S and S. They rejected it for their children's dept.

I feel well now but my whole nervous system is shattered. Sudden and terrible headaches descend on me. I live on a huge assortment of tablets. As soon as the house is in order I am going to hospital for an overhaul but I doubt they will help. The day I was taken there by the police I had just been to the doctor. He said there was nothing he could do. The truth is I just often feel severely ill and I don't know what's wrong myself. It's hard to treat such a matter. Howard suffers much as I can't control harsh, irritable moods and shout at him all day for the smallest thing. It's bad because it's not anything he does but my own state of distress. If I swallow a tranquilizer tablet 3 times a day he gets by without a good beating.

Bessie

[48]

Dear Randolph,

Gollancz has bought my short novel of 30,000 words. I wrote it first for the children's dept. of S and S but the contents made the little lady there spring out of her skin. David Machin liked it from the word go. Rare. He is careful, business-like. Then Gollancz wants to bring it out on its own. They would not have done this had it not been damn, blasted good. They are printing 1,500 copies and sending me £150. The title is *Maru*, a Tswana word meaning the elements. Gollancz let me know that they are re-printing *Rain Clouds*. I asked them to send me a copy of the second printing. They said the sales were damn good that side. I shall try to sort this matter out because they had ordered a very small re-print indeed — maybe not more than 1,000. Rejoice with me. My short novel is a bomb. But I did not expect the Gollancz offer!!

I'm going to take a holiday.

Bessie

[49]

Poste Restante, Serowe
6 January 1970

Dear Randolph,

I went to the bank and they told me that the cheque I sent you came through on the 26th November, 1969. That was a damn long time as I sent the cheque to you on the 20th

October. Now what is your bank doing that side? Please try to find out. Did I not tell you that all this business fills my mind with agony?

I wrote you a very depressed letter [47]. The clock winds down so drastically that I get a very clear impression of dying. It pains me when I think of all the good times, those oceanic phrases which pound through my head, the 8th book with the name *Thunder* and how I get from here to there. At that time I had received a letter from a friend in America and he is so eager to take some of the burdens off my life. I straight away offered him Howard, not being sure whether I would get out of my various, slow-churning agonies. I got hold of a certain gentleman today and gave him a good kiss on the cheek (because he is married) and that lightened my dismal mood. I was getting out of practice about kissing but I see that I am not so bad. There's several holes in my teeth as there is no dentist here and this prevents me from increasing my good mood as I think the gentlemen might not like to be kissed by someone with holes in their teeth in case such person has a terrible odour.

Look here I have a nice friend in America. His name is Thomas Carvlin. He is married with 8 children and a good wife. He is news editor of the *Chicago Tribune* ... When I say I love someone absolutely, I mean those people assure me of being so sane they just have to survive eternity. I know only two, you and he. The other gentleman loves me more than you do and is such a sucker for anything I say or need that I know I can be sure of just asking him. But he's far. You are sure to know first thing if I go round the bend or something so please if that ever happens relay my off-spring to him. For one thing, I have learnt bitterly and deeply that some things are beyond my control. I am simply victimised by them and there is no such thing as saying: God help me. I don't want to die. I don't want to go mad. You just do. Life is that lonely. There is no way in which you can imagine that you are so important that anyone or anything can help you. Take that as a fixed fact. I like the little boy to go on and when I get on to someone like Tom Carvlin I think he can make space for my son. I don't really care what happens to me. I have never really lived with my two feet on this god-dam earth. Yes, if the heart soars. I always made it but there's the unpredictable and the unpredictable and the unpredictable.

Of course the whole good mood today comes from kissing a certain gentleman. Why didn't I think about it before? I have an inhibition unless gestures are spontaneous and afterwards I thought a lot about the condition of my teeth. I have to go to Zambia and get my teeth fixed up so I ought to enquire tentatively from certain sources, if women with bad teeth are usually kissed, etc. All this time I have been plaguing my mind with universal problems. It must be they which are driving me round the bend and it might be a time to think about some material matters.

As ever, Bessie

[50]

Poste Restante, Serowe
19 January 1970

Dearest Randolph,

You must really be my papa. So much you say is true, especially the zoom part. What a nightmare I have been through, as though I were being slowly choked to death. It's been going on the whole of 1969, and I nearly died during the last spell. I couldn't afford to go to hospital. Things seem all right with me now but it relieves me to know that Howard would be in good care. You are sure to meet my American friend and his wife one day as you are an inseparable part of my life and he loves me. I told him most of the trouble. He gets so wild he just wants to go and "scalp" anything which harms me but how do you scalp depression? You owe me such a lot of money and *New Africans*. Please airmail me the Makeba and Mbiti review. I re-read the Mbiti review not so long ago. God knows how I wrote it with my mind breaking. Or how I have survived the worst nightmare on earth.

David is to send me £75 for *Maru* soon and I expect some royalties. But since I like money send me what you owe me when you are rich. Bye Papa.

As ever, Bess

P.S.: The books are welcome as you know.

[51]

Poste Restante, Serowe
25 January 1970

Dear Randolph,

I have received a letter from K saying she received the money. I am going to reply to her letter. I tell you she did not give a damn about anybody on this earth except herself, least of all the God she married. I hit her such a bomb, in desperation, not thinking anything would make a difference to her selfishness but it's strange she stuck on writing letter after letter to which I did not reply. I feel she has reached the stage now when I can give her one more truth and end the matter between us. You have no idea how exposed you get through people who contact you in this writing business and I have acquired some armour and protection from the sorrow she caused in my life, because balanced side by side I have got some terrific people on my list, like the Carvlin man. Also if anyone just writes to David asking for my address, he won't give it, only he will let me know.

Randolph, again I say I could not help involving you. There is so much I can carry on my own, after all I brought myself up. There was no one there. But a time comes when you reel so badly you have to get help. I just would not have lived this long, without Howard, that's all because life or death are an indifferent matter to me. People who only 'take it' look with strange eyes on people who only 'grab it' and you just don't care for the grabbing show because the performance of the grabbers is so horrible.

I'd not have mentioned in the first place that there was so little left of my mind, except that I wanted you to take the child. Dennis Brutus once wrote, 'Let the worst happen now, as the near-worst has so often happened.' Perhaps his words are deeper than he thinks because I feel that is a state of mind which creates total unselfishness and total unselfishness might be the ideal for a future experiment, especially in regard to the African situation. The dross burns up so fast here, unlike elsewhere that a day will come when there will only be the 'take its' left and we might be forced to carry immense burdens for the future.

It humiliates me to say I need help or affection but sometimes I have to say it. As for my slow churning agonies, they have too much of an involved mental climate. I got a fixed nightmare behind me. There was a woman in my dreams torturing me. She was a black woman, as though I had no right to live on this earth in my own complexion. There was a mocking smile on her face as though nothing I could do would ever make up for the crime of my complexion and such a horror overcame me that I had to put myself to sleep with tablets. I kept on struggling against the pull down, I kept on writing things opposite to the horrors and horrors of my dreams and the more I pulled up, the more terrifying the nightmares became. The way my head bust up! There was not a foothold anywhere and I had absolutely no return guns for the mocking smile and the one-way torture. It was so horrible, and so damaged me mentally, I seem to have a huge pain in my head that is so sore I could scream and scream and scream. Why do you suffer so much only to come to a simple conclusion that a world based on complexions is an empty and unimaginative world. It can't see anything beyond that, just one track: 'If you are not my complexion, you ought to die.'

There's a little boy here who likes my son. He has big blue eyes. His family is at Swaneng. Each morning he comes to fetch Howard. He says: "Don't worry about me, I've already had my breakfast." It is said with such a quaint air, of an old, old man. The first few times I laughed to myself. Then I thought: "Goddam this child is making me sane again." In such a mad world he comes out with a nice line like that.

As ever,
Bessie

[52]

Dear Randolph,

Thank you for the card. Howard likes it. Your friend Betty Sleath sent me *The New York Review*. Will you thank her for me? I shall enquire at the bank about the cheque I sent you.

I have not much news. Life is a round of depression and some gardening work; mostly the depression troubles me. If I could pull out, there is a year of good work ahead. I felt it with that short novel *Maru*, which Gollancz bought. We are still having to work on touching it up; but it should be out in the Spring of 1970. A lot of it is about the Masarwa or Bushman tribe; from the view of oppression, suffering — but it is a wide swing at all forms of racial hatred. Things I said cover everyone's suffering. Think that's why Gollancz bought it *so* quickly. Victor Gollancz was a Jew. The Gollancz people know a lot of my difficulties, the breakdown, etc from Naomi Mitchison. I am not happy, really and barely surviving. It's just to tell someone, but I may pull through. Would you look after Howard? I could get him also to people in America.

Bessie

[53]

Poste Restante, Serowe
9 February 1970

Dear Randolph,

The review you sent in *Nigerian Opinion* is great, great, great, Hardly expected such a reception. Look at that — he says — "'The God with no shoes' is turning up in the obscure parts of Africa."

Gollancz want to change the title of *Maru*. They say English people that side won't like it. I wrote back saying I am not only writing for the white man. Some of the type-script was also messed up during editing.

Considerable mental confusion my side. Last week I dated several letters 14th February. I reel to-day to find out it's the 9th Feb. Reason?

My garden is shaping up well. Onions have been transplanted. I got lost in work that side and forget time and date. I feel much better now and am slowly pulling out of the tablets, though an anxiety makes me buy some for bad days. I meant to say how sorry I was about M. You know, his mother divorced, re-married and just chucked him out of the house. He was always a frightened child who tried to be brave. Thanks for the review.

Bessie

[54]

Dear Randolph,

It is now with great joy that I remember that the NA still owes me four pounds, four shillings for the reviews I did entitled: "Remote Lives." I failed to get an American sale for *Maru*. They won't touch it because it pricks like hell over the racial question. I asked David to give it, with no sale, to one of my former editors on *Rain Clouds*. He had to push *Rain Clouds* in. The owner of S &S did not want it.

You know, I turned up with no royalties this season, except the seventy five pounds from an advance for *Maru*. The plumbing bill is as high as the sky. The bank says I owe them money as I made out one cheque too big. I knew it would happen like that though my book here shows that I ought to have about one pound ten left. Before I made out the last cheque, I checked with the buggers, now they are charging me interest so that they say I owe them R2.50! It is enough to make one's hair stand up and I doubt I shall ever make out a cheque; except a cash one. It will be a mighty crisis which will make me go through this nightmare again!

You know, I won't be lost if I had to come to England for a short while. There's a certain girl there who loves me to perishing reality. Her name is Paddy Kitchen. She did two write ups on *Rain Clouds*, one a review and one a general piece on African writing. The third thing is an interview she conducted by post with me but I got to know that her company would be fine for eternity. I could not move out of here without any money and how could papers ever get fixed up? Who would give me a passport? Some diplomatic circles in Africa are fuming. They say the Botswana government ought to deport me. They were expecting it from the advance publicity of *Rain Clouds* and some of my *New African* writing which does not soft soap Africans. I heard this by letter. They are smaller minded than the government here and just shoot people in Kenya for bugger-all so how do I get there, to England, I mean, because I can get a good welcome from Paddy Kitchen and stay in her house. I am sure of this, like the Carvlin man. Love is so rare that you know when you find it, and I have got some terrific people behind me, you too. But the other details are far beyond solution. I have given them up. Everything went wrong from the time Howard was assaulted. I never seemed to recover and the nightmare was so persistent and inward-turning, in my own mind that nothing seems to wash away the horror of this racial business.

I must tell you a funny story about the little blue eyed boy. I got to adoring him so much, he had a hell of a blow up with Howard, through jealousy. He told Howard he is never going to be friends with Howard again and Howard must never talk to him again. Then whenever I see him he gives me secret little smiles from the corner of his eyes, but there is sheer murder going on here. I never knew boys fall in love at the age of four, with such vehemence and possessiveness. Howard, who is sane and widely loved by mankind in general was much put out. He said: "I am not going to talk to Oliver again because he insulted me." So the situation remains like that. It is a little beyond me as I have never been loved by a four year old before and don't know what to do. I throw up my hands in despair!

As ever,
Bessie

[55]

Please Note: New Address. P.O. Box 15, Serowe
14 March 1970

Dear Randolph,

Has it ever occurred to you that you might one day be the cause of my wearing glasses? Glasses might make me look more noble and dignified than I really am, but look at all I'm going to miss seeing — like handsome gents. People who wear glasses really see no further than their noses. Or do you really like your letters to go half-read? A great letter writer like I, am ashamed to number you among my correspondents. One day you will have such top secret information to disclose and no one will understand.

It has also occurred to me that the longer I write for the *New African*, some of my greatest prose pieces, mind you, the longer I shall stay in the poor house. The NA must be running a disciplinary course in poverty for writers. To tell the truth, were I flush, I would disdain to accept the money, even if you owed me one hundred pounds but I have just been thinking today about living on writing and what it does to one at times. I miscalculated my income for the year and what I really ought to be doing just now is writing some other masterpiece. I have often noticed that the need for cash and the production of a masterpiece just don't coincide with me. Money will hit me at a big off-period and genius will hit me in starvation, that is, I often get the money when I don't think I deserve it and have been lolling around for days and days thinking the most abysmal thoughts.

Randolph I could go into a long something about not running away from hell but attempting to demolish it. You're too practical minded to understand that. More simply, I wind down whole periods of my life. If most of them were sorrow, what does that matter? In fact, it seems as though some of my greatest achievements are already behind me. You might remember how I lived in Cape Town. The same theme is there, the same mockery and dislike of pompous people. Therefore I had not asked you to worry so much about me, but Howard. How much of my own life I could wind down and throw away simply because I have found some truths for the soul that make it feel secure. But there is only a small statement in a child that you might like someone else to take care of for you if you feel your hold on life is getting so slack, you might not be there the next day. I don't say it is unusual but for me the hold on life has been very precarious and I am deeply repelled by human malice, viciousness and greed. I just want to throw it back in the face of any bastard, even if they kill me. For some reason some people are just permanent sitting ducks for a persistent viciousness. I seem to have that cycle in my destiny and when you overcome one evil, a greater evil still is grinning behind your neck. I have often looked in the face of a real bastard. There is no compassion there. Such a word is unheard of to him and his like — it's just a one way story — you're such good entertainment for me, I am going on and on until you drop dead. I don't think you've been pushed to the wall like that and tortured with horrors. Perhaps too, you don't know the African environment. It is top class at creating merciless, evil and deathless cruelty.

I'm worried about Howard because he is turning out so nice these days and very much my idea of what a man ought to be like. It's been such an interesting experience, living with a little boy, like him. For one thing, he functions totally independent of me. There's something about him so queer. He often talks to me, very formally, politely as if I am a total stranger to him and of one hundred things you can tell him, he will only choose two — then live them so consciously and truthfully as though only those truths are agreeable to his mind. You just exhaust yourself with other things. He won't hear a word but what he wants — it really sinks in.

You'd say for 8 years he only picked up two things from me. He's damn scared to mention any prejudice. He'll say it but apprehensively as though I am about to blow him into the sky. The other thing was — don't take without giving something in return. The last item has produced some wonderful moments, especially since he went to school. His teacher told him some fantastic things about Jesus and what he does for children. The name Jesus is meaningless because I give him no religious instruction but the story got hold of him. He came home and told me some of the things Jesus did then he said to me: "Can I make a present for Jesus?" The same thing happened to father Christmas. He had to write a letter for toys but he never forgot to ask me: "Can I make a bird and a house and tree for father Christmas?"

That's how far I got with him, otherwise he just goes out of the house and learns what he likes. I excused myself for having no apron strings. No one tied me down. I thought the little gentleman would not be a spineless jellyfish one day,

115

when he is a man. There's a whole world I know nothing about, especially the Setswana conversations. One day I asked a visitor to translate a Setswana conversation Howard was having with a friend in the yard. The visitor burst out laughing. He said the two boys were saying: "You're a goat. You're a cow. You're a something with no hair."

It's that which kills me really. Hatred and torture may be deathless. You might say: "If I am the permanent butt of obscenity surely my ending or death may make a torturer find some other victim." You know, they'd say: "If you want to die why don't you take the child with you." I felt this around Christmas and I looked for an outlet for the child. I thought some other living human being might like a boy like that who liked to make things for father Christmas, so I thought of either you or the Carvlin man because you may end up with only such a pretty boy. I don't mean to say he's good but a truth like that — Don't only take, give something in return, is one of my achievements which makes my soul feel a little secure, no matter how I die. There were two or three other things I learnt for myself — what love is really like and what evil is really like and that evil is so powerful because it does not answer to logic or reason, that *there are men who are women in disguise because malice and viciousness are feminine qualities and that such men can kill a woman like me*, because although I look feminine and am blabber mouth enough to be feminine, I am really masculine in feeling because I make straight deals and don't understand the eternal trick of — you eat me and I eat you, that's how we play this game.

You know something funny about love, Randolph? It does not appear reasonable or logical, like evil. I am still puzzling this out.

I wonder if your practical mind can understand the above

ramble. P called by. I told him to tell you I am alright. He looked an effeminate species of an Englishman and I found talking to him real uphill work, so dull and blank was his expression, so bored and dead was his mind. Keep it a secret huh? It's one thing to say bad things, its another for them to get about.

By the way, before I get on to Paddy Kitchen, that old man Louis Armstrong has caused considerable commotion in my house here. We have an L.P. of him wearing a bow tie. This got to be a big thing with Howard. He wanted a bow tie too. I managed to buy a dilapidated bow tie at a jumble sale with clips but I am damned if I know how the bow tie is attached to a shirt. It appears as if Louis has a special front piece which goes with his posh bow tie so I would be so obliged if you could explain this matter to me as you no doubt move in circles where gentlemen wear bow ties and know the details. I enclose Howard's drawing of Louis singing "The Sunshine of Love." We're both fond of the old man and his style.

Now to Paddy Kitchen. It might be so good for you to get to know both her and her husband. I'm not sure about the husband's surname but his first name is Dulan. I have a picture of him and a little boy she had from her first husband. The man, Dulan has a nice face, kind and good humoured expression. He is in a bathing costume, with some wrinkles on his tum so he might be middle aged or so. The little boy looks like me, and I think Paddy's husband might have been a Negro, from Guyana. She never mentioned anything like that, perhaps to surprise me with the picture of a really sweet little fellow. He so resembles me in appearance with his thick hair, etc, that I was so pleased to see a little comrade. ... She says little that is personal, just sketchy lines here and there as though nothing makes her really bitter. We

117

differ only there. I can set up the loudest wail in the world about any situation with all the gory details. Otherwise, we tally on almost every other point, except perhaps her vision of love making, in writing. It's a bit too free and hair-raising for my tastes! I have two of her books. We have the same publishers, Gollancz. She has three books out. I was introduced to her through Gollancz.

As far as her writing goes, she has more fully developed what you sometimes like in me — she sprawls across a page. The words just go bounce, bounce, bounce like big whops of wind. There's another thing — you can play nice games with her. I sent her a picture about an imaginary little girl called Alice, whom I like, along with a picture of Howard. She says she put both on her mantle piece. I cut the picture of Alice out of my son's reading book. It's about children's playtime in Ghana. Then she says she likes Alice too.

The husband, Dulan, might just be the blood brother you have been looking for. The man's face so appeals to me in the photo. I have no picture of Paddy. The husband works in publishing, again she did not make the details clear. The personal just does not enter, but then she is not such a good letter writer like me. Forgive the vanity, but few people equal my letter-writing ability!!

We compared a few things. Her waistline is 30. Mine 32. She likes to keep a garden and best loves sunflowers. I had some sunflowers going too, this summer. She can't get hold of the verbs. I used to suffer like that until a little steam developed, still I am shaky like her about verbs and adjectives.

I shall send you Paddy's piece on African writing. At the moment my file is out on loan to someone at Swaneng. But I enclose one of Paddy's letters, written at Christmas time, with her address at the top. Please try to get in touch with the family. I shall visit them one day but it is more likely they will visit me. Don't worry about trying to get me out of here Randolph, I just said at the time, that if I had to die I would prefer someone like you to take Howard. You did not read my letter carefully. In another way, my frequent death moods must have made death so fed up with me that I am just not worth considering. I might have troubled death as much as I trouble you and I know what you say about me: "There she goes again." You think I don't know that you pay no heed whatsoever to anything I say. You ought to pay attention to a few things, though, especially my views on the universe. Some of them are prophecies. Or did you not know that I am a prophet of some kind, huh? My sense of humour might fool you into thinking that some of my most noble conclusions "addle your wits."

Affectionately,
Bessie

[56]

P.O. Box 15, Serowe
28 April 1970
Note my P.O. Box number.

Dear Randolph,

My angel papa (don't be embarrassed by the heavy senti-ment) I'm glad you and Gillian liked Paddy and her old man. They really seem a nice family to me. Please tell Betty Sleath not to worry over much about the money from the borehole as I also put the proposition to the Carvlin man in America. He sent me a lot of seeds recently.

I love Machin very much and would not change him for

all the agents in the world. We have perennial jokes about my poor spelling, send each other presents and no other person will take my vehement language when something goes wrong! I trained him to eat it in small bits, with some swear words. Most short pieces I have sent to *The New African* and I'm not so hot unless what I have to say is a matter of life or death. So I let David have only the full length work and he picks up any number of publishers. *Rain Clouds* has five. I think too, the long haul is better for me when I get down to it. There's too much goddam steam and it's only a full length work that lets me relax a bit. In between I have to nearly kill my head with sleeping tablets. Can't calm my head down at nights. Think till 2 a.m.

Bessie

[57]

P.O. Box 15, Serowe
18 May 1970

Dear Randolph,

Please note that my address is P.O. Box 15, Serowe. They lose mail in this country because the postal system is all mixed up. I received a very lovely letter from Betty Sleath, to which I replied in like vein. Also, the Carvlin man sent me $50 for the garden.

A certain Mr Gordon Xhallie, from the Cape tells me he knows you quite well. I met him today because we have to attend a refugee committee and he came from a village 50 miles away. Strangely, he felt so much like people I used to know in what I sometimes think of as home, whom you trusted to be normally kind and good-hearted. My mental balance is long gone round the bend, as far as people here are concerned. The perverse, the weird, the insane have dominated for too long. Such howling as I put up must have really been a shameful spectacle, especially the letters, but about two years ago I was a gay, carefree soul. To tell the truth a racial feeling never entered my mind, except towards what I called "the enemy" and even there he was too far removed from me to give me nightmares. It is different if a racial feeling is created by people and I mean African, who are also human to you. It is then that you really sort out the differences and life is not the same again for me, but a horror I may never forget. The only relief or return to normal is that I have my anonymous self again. Something really went wrong for me to be openly insulted and spat at because I know how I have always lived, which is like any other anonymous person no one notices.

There is something I am curious about, though. They are a funny crowd here. Something is wrong with the outlook of people who keep their eyes glued in transfixed fascination at a woman's stomach. I've had the longest pregnancy in history, with no man in sight. And I have fantastic sex parts which have been thoroughly and widely discussed with no one really knowing what they are like. Or for that matter, no one ever stopping to question what I might be like, that all the long *verbal* love affairs I conducted with gentlemen was only to find out if they were truthful and that these said gentlemen got the soundest tongue lashing from me and were relegated to oblivion for untruthfulness. Also, that I don't ask anyone whom I ought to go to bed with because it has already been arranged for me in heaven. I prefer the certainty of heaven to the slip-shod.

You don't have to wear the fatherly cloak so heavily, if it reminds you of approaching old age, as I haven't really noticed the lack of parents as such, but there is certainly something like "being deeply attached" to others and sometimes you wonder how such sanity asserted itself, considering what we were faced with in SA. Because everything ran against the grain of normal human affections and how one might like to conduct one's life. I hardly think one's greatest loves are to be found firstly in a family circle and certainly not in colour compartments. To have the time and the place to choose great friendships seems to me, the nearest thing to heaven on earth. There is something about some people (I found a handful) that makes you say: "They are eternal in my life," and they might not be one's husband or brother and yet a comradeship exists which is as deeply binding as love for a particular individual. I balanced these things out in my mind because any kind of betrayal of those affections seems to me the end of the world itself, so great an ideal to me is the word: Friend. I also meant that you belonged among the elect.

A great meditation falls upon my mind these days, Randolph as I am preparing myself for my first literary masterpiece. There are three or four people dominating my mind but I need only one to hold the whole story together, to dominate.

The galley proofs of *Maru* are on the way to me. The title remains.

As ever,
Bessie

[58]

P.O. Box 15, Serowe
9 June 1970

Dear Randolph,

Thank you for the Chinese special. It is hard to beat but
luckily for me I have finally acquired a pair of glasses with
enlarged lenses at the bottom, so that I can really make out
all you have written. Progress?

So much drama this end. First, something went wrong
with Pat. Because he is so much surrounded by people who
are really very much put out by his cold personality, they
say he had a nervous breakdown. He certainly turned the
school upside down for one night and a morning and had the
students running like mad all over the place because he
resigned. The authorities refused to accept his resignation. I
think the performance put up by Pat was simply that for too
long he felt no one really loved him and he has a thing about
it, he's queer about human relationships. He has ALWAYS
got himself stuck on bastards but often been harsh and off-
hand to the people who really worshipped him and believed
in his ideals and made some of his very fancy projects live.
Pat can't work a job through and is a troublesome idealist
with vague dreams, the vaguer, the better. He has always
been banged in the heart so to speak, by the bastards on his
staff, most of them have been black people, refugees, he
sheltered and who let him down by just walking out of the
job. He has also carried on a long vendetta all by himself
against the Botswana government which he dislikes. He said
he was going to resign when his teacher was deported, then
he just blew up, all of a sudden one night, but I don't think
it is a serious breakdown. He is away on holiday at the

moment with his family. He has two lovely little boys. I shall let you know the end of this story.

Can you throw more light on that Nongqawuse story (see pp. 139–140)? I used to hate, deeply, the smirking white historian view of our school history books, like that is just what the natives would do. They had begun to hate the white man. I have felt it myself on another level. A bombardment of persecution, which is so illogical, makes one eventually feel 'Why don't I die.' There is also a deep mystique in the tribe. Sometimes, leaders were giants, like Hintsa. Someone told me, on his death, his head was cut open and his brains taken out. He was so brainy, he was dazzling. I forget what happened to the brains. I dedicated my book to Shaka, after reading Ritter. I accept his version and interpretation, because I grew up in Natal and Zulu-speaking people are like that, they are like Shaka, having never forgotten him, that one personality stamped a mass of people with his own genius — the passion for friendship (how great were his loves) loyalty, integrity and vigour. I grew up surrounded by that atmosphere …

Randolph, I am busy with the galley proofs of *Maru*. You know, the torture and conflict in my heart will never end. I tell you I hate everything here, but when you read the stuff I have produced in this country, the contradiction is so obvious. The title really justifies the story. I have been re-reading with transfixed attention and the main lead character really gets a hold on the mind. The book could have had no other title, he is so powerful, from the point of view that he expresses my most sound and coherent views on the question of racial oppression. I twisted my face in agony. Why did I give my most beautiful lines and experience to a Motswana when they all spat at me for being Coloured? Why did I do it? Who cares? I wanted you to see what I had worked out about racialism. I may get a spare galley from Gollancz and shall

124

post it to you because I wish I had not written *Maru* after all. It is personal and brings back many bad memories. But you may say that the story transcends the personal and can be useful. I wanted to untangle myself from it because they might say again, in error, "Bessie Head, the Motswanan" and I shall end up in hospital again with another nervous break-down, because I couldn't get out of here and most of my dreams were so long distance, the reality being the opposite. I am sick of being hated for shit and junk by illiterate tribal bastards. Damn God! Damn the future! Damn me too!

Bessie

P.S. I am not so depressed as I sound. I think, like Pat, we have no home or anything solid to get a grip on. The causes are too far ahead, for the children and me live with no love, no hope; but we work all the same, you are forced to be generous.

P.S. I shall try to get someone to take a picture of the house, with the vegetable garden too. It's pretty.

P.S. One is never sure the world will change, least of all of the power of the written word. *Maru* upsets me. My writing is a real service; useful. *Maru* ought to liberate the oppressed Bushmen here overnight.

[59]

P.O. Box 15, Serowe
3 July 1970

My Angel Papa,
I told you your handwriting would ruin my eyesight.
Think of all I'm going to miss seeing.
Like handsome gents!

As ever,
Bessie.

[60]

P.O. Box 15, Serowe
16 July 1970

Dear Randolph,

The name plate arrived today and enclosed please find a letter for Tomoichiro Okuie who made it for me. It is an understatement to say that I love it very much and also an understatement to say "thank you" to you. No postman comes my way, so it might seem to have no purpose but somehow I cried a little and became very absent-minded, muttering to myself in a distracted way. I used to like walking down the streets of Cape Town, reading all the names on the houses. I forget the name of your house, but it seemed to be something to do with the sun, wasn't it?

The name plate is with Martin Kibblewhite whom I mentioned in the letter to Okuie. Martin recently returned from England but I'd known him and his wife four years ago. The gentleman can make an adventure out of anything and his eyes twinkled like anything at the sight of the nameplate. Don't worry about it staying weather-proof and undamaged. He sees to those details because he designs houses and I thought I'd better take it to him because once he came round and examined my seedling nursery and said I had built it the wrong way, over-looking the prevailing wind and the south-wester. He knows about the wind in Botswana and houses for plants should be as carefully designed as houses for people, otherwise the south-wester will damage the plants, which it did. So when he puts up the name plate he will see what will damage it before-hand. He said to me: "I am going to remove two screws each on the dragons and put in four long screws and a plug on the door."

In my last letter I mentioned that Pat had some trouble but he has pulled through and is a changed man. None of that morose gloom of doomsday on his face. He is relaxed and happy but he does not appear to be running the school and stays mostly in his house. As you know, Swaneng is not only a school but also a development workshop and he started so many projects, the teachers say he wants to leave the school and run his projects. I had to see him the other day about the garden, etc., and I have never had a nicer and more reasonable conversation with him as though the explosion turned him into a normal, relaxed human being. We are carrying on a long argument about the garden — you know, make it financial with all the capitalist tags. He says no. It must be voluntary work with no money involved. I just looked at him and said nothing because the seed order I have made came to R15.00. The fence to R50.00 and all that money I made with a few women so we own the property with no debts. The explosion failed to turn him into a practical-minded capitalist, I'm afraid. Indeed, I am practical. I also appear to have a certain amount of control over my chequing account at the bank. I therefore smiled at this airy-fairy, dunderhead idealist and thought: "He doesn't know that I shall quietly go on making my vegetables and seedlings earn money, so much so that one day it supports all my gardeners."

Last week I turned 33. A month before I gained control over the workings of a bicycle. The two go together as far as my birthday is concerned because for some years my waist-line was keeping pace with my age e.g. 30 years old — waist-line 30; 31 years old — waistline 31; 32 years old — waist-line 32. Bang went the order this year! Age 33 — waistline 31 1/2. It's the bicycle. But more. There's a blue sky over-head and little pathways and the wind in my hair. What a life! That's why the lady is a tramp! *Bessie.*

127

[61]

Dear Randolph,

Thanks so much for the short note. The ship's rocking badly this side again: Please don't forget your promise to haul out Howard from this God-awful HELL! There's so much happened so terrible — the least I can say is that I got thrown off the garden project after working on it for 9 months. I am not well and not functioning normally. You know the old story of the trapped rat in a sinking ship. It's so enraged it just snaps at everything. You will take my child, please, Randolph. I'll be alright this side of hell but I don't want Howard to go too.

Bess

[62]

Dear Randolph,

Just received your illegible Nongqawuse letter. I make a few notes!

a. The whole thing might have started off as a psychological protest. Think of the type of white man African people encountered then - they, the "round the Cape explorers" at that time were not the best of European society; but the roughest, the most crude, blind. Now I have had some strange dreams myself due to acute emotional disturbance. People were prepared to do anything to relieve themselves

128

of a fearful presence (perhaps whom they could not compre-hend) fearful too in the sense of those weapons of now. It is at times like this that the sub-conscious dominates. (It did in Nazi Germany. Hitler had visions.) A whole nation will fall for a vision, under stress. The visions are inaccurate, because of emotional turmoil. Visions or sub-conscious per-ception need GREAT mental and emotional detachment, also a slow unfoldment; and is really the priority of saints who want nothing in particular from mankind, except to observe the VERY slow unfoldment of the sub-conscious process. *Now* the prophet saw the sun rise the wrong way and other things that made him order people to slaughter cattle. I suggest he misinterpreted the visions. The presence of the white man was simply reversing all their processes of living. What human nature *cannot* accept is the intensity of suffering that often accompanies a reversal. Then there is a blank upstairs — I mean the old man, God. You don't figure him straight in acute agony. So I'd say everything started off genuine and was grabbed as a life line by a distressed people. The fact is one *can* have visions of a future. I had private views myself of poverty themes which I mentioned to you and wrote much about but I am a *saint*, detached observer, in essence, with a soft, careless hand. I care not what hap-pens though I'd say I was Nongqawuse's uncle in a sense.

What I say to you though is that a nation in distress grabbed at one man's dream and he interpreted his vision/dream inaccurately. I know about the hair-breadth disaster of the sub-conscious. But with me it was a *gigantic* poverty theme which pre-occupied my imagination alone and never really disturbed others. Even everything I said was gentle, tenta-tive. Therefore, the inaccuracy of the prophet's interpreta-tion of his vision's comes out in Nongqawuse. She is a typical African woman, whom I dislike intensely. She jumps at the band wagon of any sensational story and makes it ridiculous. No wonder the history books *laugh*. The laugh comes with the "Victoria Regina." She'd risen, through the sensation of the prophecy to something like Queen Victoria — after all, all the white people wanted to *hear*. It must have been an appalling show. I think the uncle had a vision. The white man was a spoke in a slow, churning wheel to make things move. The spoke is *painful* but only a saint accepts and knows this. The saint too often shuts his mouth, knowing life a little too deeply.

Bess.

Maru comes in January.

P.S. I am unhappy, ill. I have a breakdown again. I'll pull out soon.

[63]

P.O. Box 15, Serowe
12 October 1970

Dear Randolph,

Let that K woman go and fry her shammy socialist and capitalist guts in hot oil. She phoned you because of that *Times* article. She's not normal. She does not like the publicity. It ought to go to her because she's so brainy and original. If you have seen as many sick human souls as I have, you'd be repelled.

I read your letter my Papa, then I went to look at myself in the mirror, (a very rare event). I can't believe I am, as you say, young, attractive and brilliant. But you always arouse my sense of humour, so to speak, at the wrong time. Certain states of slight emotional disturbance startle you into the unexpected. I have a long memory of all you said to me:

Don't be bigoted. Don't swear at God. Don't swear at that respectable old gentleman shuffling down the road. He's the keeper of society's morals. Don't show off. Keep your mouth shut while important people are talking. Have a social conscience ... and so on. When have your efforts to make me respectable EVER succeeded? Now suddenly you say something so nice, quite out of touch with reality as one has to live it. You know, I don't care whether it is the Queen of Sheba or who, all the goddam female species think they've got more than I've got. The way they swagger their blasted backsides in my face! I was concentrating on other things. You also know Randolph that I would never dream of pinching another woman's husband or boy, don't you? I'm so good. If you ever dare say young, attractive to me again, God knows, I'd be tempted to vanity and get like these rotten females whom I despise. I dismiss the compliment but it amused me, thinking of you and what you usually come out with in a state of slight emotional disturbance. Your heart must be normally very peaceful, my Papa.

Indeed, my nervous breakdown is not functioning the right way and I am well aware of it. Irrelevant things like organising a garden and getting blocked by a small mean person ticks off that falling to pieces sensation. Too much of my life depends on a capacity to sustain solitude but I can balance this with activity, often blind and determined and move so fast I don't have time to look hard at a man like Pelotona and other bad hats. I can't see the crooked and small and mean because I don't believe in it and it is too infantile and purposeless. That is just where I get unhooked all the time in a bog of the vicious, cruel and mean because I can't equal it. It takes me time to pull myself together and during that time I always think I won't make it.

... Pat said to me: "Trouble really revolves around you.

131

You aren't easy to get on with." He meant so much more because he deeply respects me, in spite of us never really liking each other. He understands consistent decent behaviour because he is, from observation, one of the very few men whose behaviour is consistently decent. It makes him do the hardest things. It makes me the kind of female who would rather hang myself than be a clinging wall flower. Randolph, Pat protected me for more than six years in an aloof, cold way. There was never a time he did not assist me but only towards making the most difficult decision. That is how I have survived this long. God, the Abstract, whom I have served, perhaps unwillingly, will grant me a favour and make that man my eternal brother. I need him. He's like you. You both force me to efforts, and don't seem to care if they hurt me.

Bessie

P.S. Publication Date of *Maru* was postponed to Jan. to coincide with Penguin's edition of *Rain Clouds. Maru* is a MASTERPIECE! I know it. It will liberate the Bushman.

[64]

P.O. Box 15, Serowe
21 October 1970

Dear Randolph,

I received a letter from Cleo McNelly. She said by way of introduction: "I am Randolph's friend." That was the first line. I looked at it in utter disbelief because I though I'd written a letter like that and it back-tracked to me. I mean I'm so used to that line. She then apologised for being white, middle class, American; like she had got the works from life. I said in reply it no longer counted to me that I'm black but it counted if I was good. Randolph, I have to mention something. If it is irrelevant to me, the race, I am, I'd be very anxious to know, since I adopted you, if it is your unconscious habit to walk around thinking: "I'm Randolph, the white man, perhaps upper class." I put aside my black skin because it's childish, though I was not prejudiced like the Boers. Cleo McNelly strikes me as a goddam nice woman from her first letter. She is not so sure of herself like the rest of the females. I like her.

Sincerely,
Bessie

[65]

P.O. Box 15, Serowe
22 October 1970

Dear Randolph,

I don't know much about the 1904 Herero refugees except what I heard from R's wife, who was my friend when they were here. The Rs were very secretive. Was told the Hereros were settled on the Ngamiland border of Botswana, as a community and cattle raisers. The women wear the long dress, very much like the Xhosa women of Transkei. Not a national or African costume, really, said R's wife, but introduced by the missionaries. Once R's wife said Herero's were *so* dumb politically — but then I could not follow *her* politics either. It was a mixture of UN intrigue and the devil. I used to question her a great deal about men, babies and food on which she had a tremendous amount of information. She was half mad politically and I survived in her company because the stories about the three essentials of life used to always leave me with my mouth wide open. If I'd really been interested in the Hereros, I'd have been a spy. The Rs are *that* mad. It was the memory of other things that made me so violently love R's wife. One day I said I'd write something about Hereros as she once, very cautiously, gave me a description of their journey to Ngamiland. She jumped up the wall. Hereros were *top* secret. God the way I swore at her!

Bess

[66]

P.O. Box 15, Serowe
16 January 1971

My Angel Papa,

I have been ill for about three weeks now. So terrible was it that I lost track of the days and lived through a long nightmare of darkness. There was a story of getting hold of a certain old lady who had it coming to her and knocking her soundly on the head with my fists. But in between there were complete blanks. The times when the darkness cleared up a bit, I kept on picking up your letter and roaring with laughter. I kept on saying: "What is the world coming to? MY PAPA going the church *every Sunday*?" Do you have a secret love affair on your mind, my dear Papa? I have heard that it is often love affairs that drive men to God, in desperation. In any case, in between being ill, I kept on rising to the surface and roaring and roaring with laughter.

You will excuse me. You know, from my writing and letters that I have a tremendous enthusiasm for God, in general. There isn't anything that I cannot and will not say about God. The times I mentioned God to you, you wrote back very reproving letters. You said: "Your version of God addles my wits. Don't presume to lipread God. Be very careful not to swear at God ..." and so on. When I received these letters, I left off direct conversations with God to you, but everybody else got those conversations I invented for God and many a letter examined God from side to side. About God, I never lack material.

I don't know how long it's been going on but I think I can say, with authority, that God in the end, is not an old man in the sky or invisible, but certain living individuals whom I adore. Then I'd throw you into the lump too. The mistake is to pray to the invisible. I never have. I have prayed to living things I can see. I distrust what I cannot see. When those individuals failed me I always said: "Wait, B. Head, you will soon see another God." That's my view of God. God is either people or I am not interested. My Papa, I'll never be caught dead in a church, so sure am I that God ought not to be invisible.

About Jesus I have much to say, in a way that would surprise you. Can you wait until you get a book from me entitled: JESUS. It is far too complicated to explain in a letter but a book will have to do to explain the pros and cons about him, especially the cons, they far outweigh the pros. After you have read my book, you'd then decide about the divinity in any God. Divinity seems to suggest an untouchable holiness. I distrust that. There is no such thing. There is hard living, great blunders and great abdications and the people who make these lives of immensity and history are the Gods.

Don't you worry about Hilary Rubinstein. When David Machin left A. P. Watt, I straight away set to work to make him eat out of my hand and I have got the gentleman down to a state of abject adoration. First I sent him the article on Naomi Mitchison. It turned out he really loved her. Then you know *Maru* is my masterpiece. He got a man at McCalls in New York to buy *Maru* . Then Heinemanns Educ. Series also bought *Maru*. God knows, that short bit of literature is so goddam beautiful, it is the best thing I've written so far, in very adverse circumstances. I mean I wrote it right in hell. It glories *friendship* between a man and a man and friendship between a woman and a woman. That is the base. Everything is worked out from there. I have the final product, the book right here. I keep on holding it to my heart. Randolph, it is a goddam beautiful book, like nothing else on earth. I am getting five copies from Gollancz this week, I think, and I shall air mail a copy to you right away. The major theme is racial oppression and a hard look at it but it is blended and blended and was written with a real glow.

As ever,
Bess

3 FRANCISTOWN-SEROWE: 15 January 1969 – 16 January 1971

Much of the substance of *A Question of Power* (1973) began to appear as Bessie lived her "perpetual breakdown" after the *Rain Clouds*-induced euphoria had worn off. There is the lift with the building of her first house and my own minuscule contribution of a nameplate, carved by Tommy Okuie, a young Japanese illustrator employed by my firm. Somehow, throughout her "slow, churning agonies," she managed to work, producing the plan for a new book, marked in red pencil, for my comments (nowhere to be found, even in my memory) and the writing of *Maru*. Of her book reviews in *The New African* (March and November 1969), that of J.S. Mbiti's *African Religions and Philosophy* earns its place in her collected writings, with its celebration of the simple, communal religious ideas of Africa, as "wide and generous enough to take in all the humble, who shall, one day, unexpectedly, inherit the earth".

Her reviews of Tayeb Salih's *The Wedding of Zein*, a collection of Yoruba short stories, and *Potent Ash*, stories by Kibera and Kahiga were brief and penetrating, especially the last, which was painfully so, producing a hurt response from the publishers. The Mbiti review was her last for *The New African* which, after nine troubled years, was not to appear again. Bessie had been a frequent contributor from the seventh issue and "Things I don't like". It was her only published poem and was very much of her "soap-box" period. She later rejected both soap-box and verses. The stories have appeared over and over again in anthologies and in collections of her work, not always attributed (as with "Looking for a Rain God" in *The Collector of Treasures*, 1977).

Rain Clouds and, as much, her correspondence and encounters with writers and journalists led to press articles which heightened public awareness of so unlikely a figure as a young black woman writer in remote Botswana. *The Times* columnist, PHS, in January 1969, announced the forthcoming *Rain Clouds* and coined for Bessie the epithet "exuberant" (to become, in Gollancz's publicity material, "ebullient", to which she objected.) The book, PHS quoted her, would leave her "swimming in more money than I need — I'll buy a caravan, and I'll fry sausages in the bush, and I'll make coffee". PHS's paragraph ("Success for Durban orphan") was flanked by stories about Jan Palach, the self-immolating Czech hero, and a Pilgrims' dinner attended by Wilson, Home, Heath, Thorpe and many of the British great and good of those days.

In the only English review which pleased her, Dominic Le Foe gave almost half his 1,000 words to *Rain Clouds*, the rest shared by three substantial novels, including a new Pakenham. It was the sort of review most authors would dream of — and most publishers' copywriters, packed as it was with quotable accolades. Le Foe ended: "Her book is not only a fine literary performance, it is a remarkable service performed for her race. Its publication may well be remembered as a moment of significance in the evolution of modern Africa and her relationship with the rest of the world. It deserves that distinction" [39].

Another article, in late 1970, was the product of a correspondence with an English writer, Paddy Kitchen, who, after reading *Rain Clouds*, had asked Bessie for an "interview by post". *The Times Higher Education Supplement* gave it three columns, and, like PHS, used one of John Goldblatt's appealing photographs of Bessie — piercing-eyed, in full flow of conversation, with that questing air (see p. 5). Kitchen included brief shots, from Bessie's letters, of her characters — like the real-life Makhaya of *Rain Clouds*, seen studying in her "shack in the buṣh", and the woman instructor in the Farmers' Brigade in *Power*. The story of her birth and early life was told: "I did a lot of my own upbringing ... I would not be the universe had I had a family life with all its narrowness. I am happy". Another letter ended "My mother is my private goddess, I alone adore her". Paddy Kitchen and, until his tragically early death, Dulan Barber, became loyal friends and Paddy her literary mentor.

Was it the *The Times Higher Education Supplement* "interview by post" that, as Bessie thought, prompted K to telephone me? K was unlikely to have seen it, but it was a year since *The Times* diary paragraph.

Those of my own letters which Bessie kept were hurried, laconic, and too often written rattling in and out of London on commuter trains, turning my already crabbed hand into "Chinese" [58]. They aimed always to sustain and inspire her, to urge her to write. She knew this and wrote of Van Rensburg and me: "You both force me to efforts and don't seem to care if this hurts me". "Seem" was the right qualifier. I tried to help her prepare her mind for the troughs that always lay ahead of the peaks: "You seem to be on a perpetual rollercoaster and I can only pray you will go zooming up again and that the next downward path will not give you the pain you seem to be suffering now". My letter ended: "I hope I am right that you are in an upturn as you read this. If not, please HOLD ON. You'll be all right. The good outweighs the bad", and with Browning's lines from "Asolando": "Held, we fall to rise, are baffled, to fight better, sleep — to wake" [50].

Her major crashes might be heralded by minor upsets, like her half-serious attack of nerves over opening a bank account, which I tried to calm with Stephen Leacock's account of his own comically daunting experience. Her "I laughed a lot" was unconvincing [45].

She could write comically in the midst of her waking nightmares — sending me a (lost) comic photograph of herself in spectacles [59] — but her humour could tip over into near hysteria, as in her "roaring and roaring with laughter" at the thought of my churchgoing [66]. That exchange stayed with her until she was back from Lobatse [69, 70]. She ended the last letter before Lobatse with "business" about her new agent Hilary Rubinstein and more rather overwrought glorying in *Maru* [66]. Whether she sent me the book I cannot now recall; the copy I have has Gollancz's compliments slip in it. A few months before she had sent me the US (Bantam) edition of *Rain Clouds*, movingly inscribed.

Her view of the Xhosa cattle-killing delusion of 1857, inspired by the girl-prophet Nongqawuse and her uncle Mhlakaza, helped me in turn, in my researches on this turning-point in the African-European power struggle in South

Africa [58]. The Xhosa, after a century of frontier conflict with the Dutch and then the English, saw their world slipping away when a masterful colonial governor, Grey, set about breaking their ancient social system and turning them into a black proletariat. Their last, desperate resort was to bring back their dead chiefs and warriors and to make all things new by obeying the prophetess, who told them to kill all their cattle and plant no crops. Famine killed 200,000 and Grey had his way with the broken remnant.

In her midway position between the two races, belonging to both yet accepted, as she felt, by neither, she grasped the essence of the cattle-killing tragedy, as historians have failed to do. The agonising, long-drawn-out humiliation of the failure and aftermath of the prophecy she pin-pointed with a tiny detail that caught her novelist's eye: "No wonder the history books *laugh* [her emphasis]" — in Nongqawuse's later life she renamed herself Victoria Regina. But after all, "the white man was a slow, churning spoke in a wheel to make things move" [62].

The search for her when she was in Lobatse mental hospital brought at last replies from Van Rensburg and the medical superintendent. Naomi Mitchison shed more light on her delusions, which will puzzle biographers, like:

> her idea of a plot against Quet Masire [prime minister of Botswana], whom she supposes to be dead. The fact that I had seen him was quite pushed aside. She knew she was the victim of a plot by Seretse and she goes about saying so. I tried hard to persuade her that her real life and fantasy life should be disentangled, but it was no use.

Patrick van Rensburg wrote in June 1971 that she had been visited only infrequently, Lobatse being several hundred miles distant and Bessie unwilling to see most of those wishing to help her:

> This seems to be the nature of her illness and always has been over the last eight years — continually alienating those who take an interest in her and try to help. According to the psychiatrist at Lobatse, she may remain in hospital for two or three years.

He asked that we in England try and get her into the country for treatment, though he was certain she would never be allowed to return:

> because of certain unfortunate statements which she has made concerning the President. It is only due to the greatest tolerance and compassion that she is being allowed to remain in the country at all, and that she has not been prosecuted for her actions ...

Patrick's ending made me realise how painful the whole matter was to the Van Rensburgs and others in Botswana, even more than his remark that I had "shown considerable interest in Bessie's welfare, *at a distance* [my emphasis], over the last eight years":

> Randolph, what more can I say? The situation, as we have control over it here, is grim. There is very very little that we can do and we feel very sad and helpless.

Six days later Bessie wrote: "I've just got home. I was locked up in a loony bin for nearly three months" [67]. Her letter crossed with mine to Lobatse Mental Hospital, to which the psychiatrist replied at once that Bessie had "fully recovered" and had been discharged.

4. Serowe (2)
29 June 1971 - 3 May 1975

[67]

P.O. Box 15, Serowe
29 June 1971

Dear Randolph,

I've just got home. I was locked up in a loony bin for near-ly 3 months. Howard is alright.

The truth is I'd lived in a sort of nightmare here for a long time. By end of 1970 I was so broken I could hardly walk. I broke down and poured out the torture in incoherent fash-ion. I got locked up. At first I just felt relief to seem to have thrown off the horrors that haunted me. But I broke my life here. I am sorting out what to do as the next best thing. I have a little money to keep me going. Howard is alright. Remember I kept on asking you to take care of him? It was that nightmare life. It went on and on with no end and it stemmed from the soul and others were involved. You said not to come to England. I am not sure what to do.

Bessie.

[68]

P.O. Box 15, Serowe
15 July 1971

Dear Randolph,

Thank you very much for your short note. Please do not worry about my coming to England. For one thing I am too broken down to make the move. For another I feel I have to get to grips with my situation alone. There was a time I used to write panic-stricken letters but I am well aware of one theme to the breakdown. The underlying part was death. The things I said and did at the time were a kind of final howl. They were so bad that I cannot repeat them.

Events were never normal here and I was entirely unprepared for what opened up inside me over a long period — a depth of evil without a name and a height of goodness without a name. The least you get from those good books is platitudes, without fire. People simply want to believe in an infinite goodness without examining the basic ingredients of the soul. I was unfortunate enough to do so and went insane. It is a horrible world of torture and very dangerous. I can't stand pressure over a long period and now it is hard to turn the accusing finger of destiny towards myself, that I was living hell itself and did not know or perhaps I only wanted to accept heaven, without pain. Haven't people done it for centuries and then slaughtered each other? Don't they say in South Africa that they are Christians?

Randolph, I did have a choice. What would have happened? I was not well. I was tortured beyond endurance. For one brief moment I threw myself on the ground and said: "God, help me." Then I made an error. In the same breath I said: "Which God?" As though, subconsciously I had not come to

143

the end of the road yet. That question, the pause and looking over my shoulder, unhinged my mind which was already over-burdened with suffering. I wanted to throw everything overboard in one violent breath, which I did. No one followed what I was saying. It was all an internal torment belonging to me alone. In the confusion I opened up a wide radius of pain for other people.

The loony bin freed me for a brief while from a deep overhanging sense of evil, as though I had abruptly shaken off the devil, but I am lost in a sorrow too deep for words. When I look back, as I am free to do now, there was a storm behind that gave me no peace. Why did it happen like that? Did I really have to learn so much? Because I sit with the weight of it — don't grab, don't love, don't hate, don't live, don't, don't, don't. I must have been an unusually stupid person to have so many bombs thrown at me.

A beautiful woman looked after Howard while I was in the loony bin. I was talking to her the other day. She told me that a strain, endured over a long period, blows one's personality to bits. She said she felt like that when she left Rhodesia and came to Botswana. Not so long ago we used to share spices from my garden and cookery recipes. It seemed like it was centuries ago and things I would not have thought over, careless remarks about children seem like mountains of information I know nothing about. That's how bad it is at present Randolph. I could not go to England in a state like this. There is only one human nobility left in me. I am not afraid to die.

As ever,
Bessie

[69]

P.O. Box 15, Serowe
13 August 1971

Dear Randolph,

Thanks so much for your letters. I'm not as mad and depressed as the last letter I wrote to you. At least I'm standing up on very shaky legs.

God knows how I wish I could go away somewhere. It's just not that easily done, when you have no travel documents and I have been in touch with United Nations for years, especially while living in Francistown. That song: I have to go away has been going on for years and years because all the wrong things were happening. Half of it was one man, then another man, then another man and weird versions of love in the air, accompanied by abnormal sights. *Maru* gives a good insight into the situation. I keep on looking back along the road I've travelled and seem to see no alternative to the disaster, as though it were something I had to go through with, and end. I am only crying about the people who got hurt because it was not so bad when I kept silent but once I started speaking, I said both vile and violent things because I could not endure any more torture. It is what I said that so sickens me. You know, very few people understand deep horror, fanatical possessiveness, the extremes of emotion, a kind of battle where evil is used to outwit the enemy; or if not outwit — then to sever memories. I eventually found myself pulled right down to that level. The terrible thing is that I did it all by myself when I was ill in health. No standards of nobility remained. You wouldn't understand emotional involvement like that because you refer to your better judgement but now I question love and am deeply afraid of it because its other face is evil.

You can come up against a sort of love so vehement and cruel that it is hardly fit for human society. You can find people glued to you like cement and they won't let go and the links were not made now, but centuries ago. The surprise was to pick up those links in a god-forsaken country like Botswana. Everything was here, the past and the future. I was struggling to destroy the past, knowing that it had no place in the future.

Randolph, I deeply value your care and affection and concern for me. Please don't let go of me. There is one thing I can say for myself. I have survived many impossible situations, maybe this is the worst, but I should see my way out of it too because of Howard, for one thing, and because I have learnt so much. It is like saying that really bad experiences create a new perfection. I wouldn't have known the depths of feeling if I had not been dragged down to them and disliked them. I think there is something wrong with superficial goodness and most people are protected by that. I was not allowed that covering and if in the future I say: I can harm no one, I can do no wrong — it is only because of experience, which was real in its way.

I am writing a little and this letter is very much taken from my present themes of thought — that seeing and feeling evil was of value to me, for the future.

You know, the breakdown so much involved Pat that his wife was very nervous about my staying here. I talked to her and she was afraid I would break down again. I hit one of his teachers. I have a house just outside the school fence and things aren't what they were before the crack up. I had lots of friendly people I knew. It was like approaching them and simply crying for help. "Please take away the nightmare." A lunatic does not do it the right way but the nightmare lasted for more than three years.

I wish like you say that I could leave Botswana. I don't have that much money. I also wanted to say that the war that was going on was not over B. Head, the living woman, but over the soul and its past wealth. B. Head, the living woman, had little opportunity or occasion to create any beauty, such as I saw behind me, where love was a big flare that lit up the skies and piled up great wealth (that is if you take it that the soul has a long history behind it.) I seemed to do little but be swayed this way and that by internal storms and a fierce pull and tug. There was a terrible and persistent theme of obscenity, I think mainly to break me down. I fought it for a long time and what came out over Christmas was the obscenity. What I said then would have made your hair stand on end. It was thought that I was suffering from a form of insanity not yet known on earth but then people know very little about the soul. I knew nothing until I went right through the mill and now I wonder if some years of suffering pay for centuries of hell and that it was well worth it.

Liz Van Rensburg told me she had written you an angry letter asking you to do something about my situation as they thought nothing could cure me. I think it was unease at having me around here, that caused it. From my side I knew how private was the struggle I was waging and to a certain extent I don't follow the whole process that forced it out into the open. I do nothing drastic unless under pressure that gets too great for me. Years and years of my life went in peaceful solitude, of some kind or the other.

Life is a funny thing. There are no clear warnings along the way, even for the very alert and there is something strange about the soul; it won't get relaxed and free and ungrasping unless suffering is so excruciating as to be a big howl. It is at that point that it widens out and becomes beautiful. I half wish to live a little longer because just now the churning around of thought is much more pleasing to me than it was some time ago.

We were still talking about God and church when I went to the loony bin. You said: "Be still and know that I am God." God is such a vague proposition in the heat of living and so often when I look back on what has been said, God seems to me to be the personality of individuals. I was also just taken aback suddenly about your going to church and mentioning it because we never discussed such a thing before. Also when I say the personality of individuals I mean what they work out for themselves as standards of goodness and some of these standards became universal. God knows I am wild enough to look for the God of the Anglican church: "Be Still." I have a habit of talking to something at night, just to get above myself; but peace of heart, the stirrings of wonder, the things that made the earth and the heavens glow, all came from living people. I wish the unknown God could walk in on me sometime, unexpectedly and say: "Here I am. Now love me." It might have happened to me in some other age and time but I am following through something just at a point where I am down on my knees — how much is personality because it gets you through so much and when you are really broken that's when you ought to see how you will survive.

Please Randolph, whatever else happens, keep a hold on me somewhere and please keep writing.

As ever,
Bessie

[70]

P.O. Box 15, Serowe
13 August 1971

Dear Randolph,
I can't see any other way out for me just yet. I only have

two books published and they are not much of an income for travelling and I have been in touch with United Nations for years but never succeeded in getting any travel documents. They say I can get a travel permit from immigration here. I did apply but there was no response and I am not certain about how to push the matter because I don't know where to go. So I turned to do a bit of garden work and some writing.

We were just talking about God and going to church when I went to hospital. I seemed to be wrestling with something, a swirling pattern of goodness as though it were being interwoven into the affairs of everyday life, like God was being scaled down and de-mystified. Somewhere I had you in that pattern. We had never discussed God or church going and I started laughing suddenly when you abruptly mentioned going to church and said: "Be still and know that I am God." So much that has been said of God was the tentative, and *flexible* searchings of men. Nothing was certain and fixed, though church buildings seem to be.

Just right now I am very afraid. One half of me feels that there ought to be something holy and infinite somewhere. The other half of me was pulled towards living things as though all the stirrings of wonder, the things that made the earth glow, the loves that moved and created history were to be found in living people. This dominated. I had no control over the images that came towards me, no escape from personal, living entanglements: "It's this road! It's this road! Here we kiss like this with all our mouths and bodies. We eat food. We make children. We are vehemently jealous. And yet, we are humane and tender and humorous PROVIDED if I am a man, no one wants my woman, or if I am a woman, no one wants my man." I was baffled and tortured by this because on the one hand I could clearly feel that love wasn't only sex. It was force, food, life, mystery, heaven, the uni-

149

verse and wild flowers that unexpectedly grow with the spring rain and out of all that was created the infinite, the eternal AND GOD. So persistent was this theme that I came to follow it with intent concentration. That propelled the breakdown. I was re-living my own inner code, my own inner world, with many ghostly forms of the past. If you tell one person you will love them forever, so do you tell many because that is the base of love as though it will never end. It was to break that theme, the promises, the ties and the toll it took on my health and sanity cannot really be counted up. It was a private struggle that was eventually forced into the open because the anguish had run too high. No one could understand a word of what I was saying and even today there is a huge joke going the rounds — "It doesn't matter what Bessie says because no one will believe her." I was stammering with agony because what had been heaven had another face which was hell.

Randolph, who understands feelings? People only read in the newspapers about murders, mostly over who loved whom. I began to understand a little of both sides of love — a heaven of perfection and a hell of degradation. You can't balance the two side by side, one eliminates the other and then dominates. It was as though that were the crux of the battle and preferably I want to feel that in my own struggle, only heaven was left.

If we have to live with love, in the future, we also have to live with our friends who come in to tea. That was what was being sorted out for me — who were the eternal friends and who was the lover? The process of sorting this out was basic, violent, down-to-earth, severe, shattering, with blows hurled in all directions. It ought to have remained a secret. Trouble came when I exposed a war that was simplifying the future for everybody.

I am afraid of the new song: "The kingdom of heaven is inside people." That kingdom holds greater demands of the person than celibate monks never knew. It is one thing to sit in isolation and say: God, the unseen, I worship you. It is another to say to a living man: God, the seen, I worship you. It is like loving a prickly pear and only the very sane can love like that.

[71]

P.O. Box 15, Serowe
24 September 1971

Dear Randolph,

Thank you for your letter. I put your post card above my writing desk, as perhaps a lucky omen for me. I don't think I'll manage to create "Heathcliff," "Mr Rochester" or the gentle atmospheres of Jane Austen's drawing room books. The men of my books have been too victimised by me. They are under the skin effeminate so and so's and the only way you can really strip them is how they go in for long spells of celibacy. People feel some impact, they are deliberately majestic because, so often the rhythm and flow of my feeling needs a masculine expression. I can't seem to make it feminine because the power of my own feelings is like a permanent sledgehammer blow. Nothing really softens me down. I accepted too many peaks, too many efforts, possibly too many abysses too, dominated by a fatal acceptance that such things are necessary for the soul.

I am a quarter of the way on my third book but this time I keep on waiting for the man I once again victimise to step free of me, thinking I'll never really solve the problem. I fear though he is much worse than Makhaya and Maru because he is the antidote for suffering with an unbending tenderness. I'd started three other typescripts struggling with the male lead and none of them satisfied me till I fell back on something I can't really see. I did use the other men for my own form but this time I can't feel at all what I am shaping, except a concentration of tears which I call humanity and a concentration of experience which I call love. But the main thing is to write until something emerges and then I'll go back and sharpen the first chapters. I feel the weakness there because I do have much to push out but I've not got the right feel of the personalities I am working with. I tentatively called it "Summer Flowers" but it means so much, wild wayward free gifts like the way the wild flowers grow in the bush after the rain.

There's a big leap forward for me, internally. I don't think my outward life is secure but the inside is free and I thought that if I could build on that the practical, outward problems would resolve themselves. So half my life is divided between the garden work I am doing and struggling with the new book. I enjoy the struggle with the book like a slow upward journey but it is a pain in the neck for Howard because it makes me terribly absent-minded. I can catch on to some lovely lines — "innate goodness makes a man seek tender and short-cut routes to heaven," then I don't quite know who is saying that because I have no strong control over my mouthpiece. That's what I want to say and I sometimes stand still for hours in the room struggling to find someone to say it with form and movement and joy. Somewhere in the background I hear a long moan: "I'm talking to you but you don't answer. You haven't put the button on my shirt. You haven't sewed my pants." Just the other day he hit on a comical solution of mimicking the way I talk: "Where's my blessed shoes? There's a blessed thorn in my foot." I hear because it's said in a high shrill voice.

Thank you very much for the few lines on God. Like the men in my books, I very much fear I have misused God too. What I never said God said, takes some beating. The licence, perhaps the blasphemy arose from a certainty that the shape of the universe itself was God then maybe I don't really want to use that word at all. In any case I want to try out in my third book an explanation of a person simply as part of this flow and shape and form I felt so strongly then. God help Africa, I like to say my latest observation is African. Mind you, the amount of private revolutions I've lived through here would defeat a contortionist. In the end I really am a human being but the process of becoming so has worn me out and turned my hair stark grey. It looks odd. I keep feeling I haven't washed my hair but all the time its changed from black to grey, the whole blessed head, so you can get some idea of the pressure I've lived through.

In so many ways, I am happy, not caring really about anything I formerly cared about. You do so much, or overjudge your own humanity then you get put into a position where other people have to do things for you. A trite phrase comes to mind: "Don't kick a dog who is down." That's what other people had to do for me. Someone told me I was a subject of much talk, talk, talk and I know the talk must have been awful but nothing awful was said to my face, by anyone around me. Surprisingly, a number of people pulled out breakdowns in sympathy. The amount of people who have had nervous breakdowns at Swaneng takes some beating! Nearly every house I walked into had a nervous breakdown in it, mostly women and some astonishing confessions: "I've been married twice and I'm not happy. Marital problems gave me a breakdown last year." Some people simply cooked up nervous troubles as far as I could see! But the main thing is being put on the receiving end then seeing what people do.

I got short-changed and reduced. I made a rule I hope I'll carry into my future incarnations: "Never flare up against people. Get the hell out of a tense situation and keep your hair in place."

The funny thing was that I saw the explosion coming but could do nothing to save myself. There were loud warnings from my subconscious. I heard it so clearly one night, someone saying: "There's a bomb for you. It's going to blow you up and your house too." I knew by "house," nothing of the thing I'm living in but my internal life but I did not have the brains to save myself from exposure. It is the exposure that makes me actually take out a lease on life, and really the peace I feel at present is because I took out the lease, keeping death at bay, for how long I don't really know. It changes everything and induces some odd reflections. There was something familiar. I was re-creating inwardly a past where I continually brought myself to death through sheer aggression of personality, a point where permanent foes really pressured me into death because the same hatreds flare up, and the same loves, both totally destructive but with the difference that the foes were really "wee, sleekit, timorous, cowering beasties," and oh, what I panic I set in "their little breasties." As for the loves, I'll have to evolve a new philosophy for them, for me because I tower above them too and have overcome them too, something like Darwin said, that all beautiful things ought to progress according to general laws. I am misquoting, but there's something in general laws that is quiet and steady. I read a bit of Darwin, mostly because in my next incarnation I hope to be a biologist, not a haphazard plant inspector like I am now but a real scientist, because by the time I come around again mankind will be populating Mars and the first thing they will need there is the kind of plants that can grow on Mars. So, if by chance you happen to turn up as my real father next time, be sure to encourage me to study biology. The next thing I'd like you to do in our household is suppress emotionalism, especially in me. You're sure to recognise me, in the household, for creating tempests. I hope I'll adore my mother. The other thing is that I have a list of people lined up for great friendships, both male and female, so I hope you will encourage loyalty and keeping great secrets. Some people have said wonderful things to me: "Bessie Head always reminds me of a friend I should have shared secrets with — but couldn't; a girl I would have skipped Double-Dutch with or discovered the essence of red berries, which you can eat as opposed to green berries, which you can't ..." I think that completes the list of personal requirements. Before I die I shall have sorted out the male species and what I am going to do about that because I am damn pig-headed on the question of love and have to learn to work it out by myself. It's the one area I have to gain control of and understand and it fascinates me to look at it from all sides because it is the one area of life, I feel, that makes people god-like and also creates the opposite — all kinds of horrors and evils.

As ever,
Bess

[72]

P.O. Box 15, Serowe
15 October 1971

Dear Randolph,

Thanks for the post card. I'm fine. *Maru* has been bought for filming by an independent film producer in New York. I've just sent off the contracts today. The main thing is that it relieves financial worry as I might not get the third book done so quickly but I can't imagine what *Maru* would look like as a film So much is uttered softly. Dikeledi is the only lively character there and sane. I don't know how the man will put over my cock-eyed version of love, with dazzling rainbow bloody lights in the eyes and glowing forms. It's murder. I still love the Masarwa girl Margaret. She's really the pivot of the book but many people here dislike the men very much. They've pointed out to me that they're quite horrific and not like normal decent men at all. I agree. But it was something I saw at the time and was trapped between a battle of good and evil. Goodness becomes much clearer later.

As ever, Bessie

[73]

P. O. Box 15, Serowe
6 December 1971

Dear Randolph,

Thanks for your letter and all the business news. Indeed, they, my agents, fleeced me on the money for the film contract. It's higher. 10% for novels. 15% they take for film money. They and some unknown person also took off for "foreign tax." Out of about £450 I end up with £220. I am supposed to get 5,000 dollars more once filming begins. I must query with Hilary about that "foreign tax." Yes, Hilary takes care of everything financial for me.

Ah! So you like the gents in *Maru*. Well, people have tended to associate the book with the breakdown. HA, HA, they really thought I had a real, live Maru and Moleka in my life and out of genuine sympathy came and told me very seriously that men like Maru and Moleka are no damn good. That's only I'm mad; etc. I was caught off-balance. Everything I had thought and felt lost its validity. But the struggle with the third book threw me back to the 2nd book. There are things there that are *valid* and *solid* goodness. There is a *strong* control over the people Dikeledi, Maru and Moleka. I dominate them mentally and that was my power. I was right on top and dictated the terms of generosity which makes the evil in Maru and Moleka *nearly* impotent. But they had a dark stream of evil and my unease about them clearly comes through. The other thing about Maru was that he was 3/4 part me; coherent, understood with a clear strong outline, though if I were a man I'd be more in temperament and behaviour like Moleka. I love the devil-may-care. Maru is feminine reasoning with a few masculine stop gaps. The funny, funny thing is that what I look on as effeminate strikes over as man, separate, individualistic, dominant; at least from the reviews — that's true maleness, they say. I thought the crux of it is me. I'm really a man with a skirt on. The other thing I've found is that Africa is basically a masculine culture.

Bessie

[74]

P.O. Box 15, Serowe
28 January 1972

Dear Randolph,

Don't know if you know a *very* pretty girl called Jackie. She teaches at Swaneng and just yesterday told me she had come back from London and failed to see you. She went on holiday there with the Hoffenbergs. You're such a homely type with the bits and pieces of clutter you gather around yourself that I did wonder how you were making out in that very foreign land. Well, would you like to *share* the B. Head fame? *Maru*, for instance is roaring on to the bestseller list in England. Gollancz told me. They forced me into setting a deadline for the third book and I said July. I'm typing like hell this side to meet the deadline. They may reject it. It's bloody complicated. But on the off-chance that they accept *could I dedicate it to you*? You know in many ways it's you who are my writing mentor — the freedom of thought and mental stability you brought out via *The New African*, and this piece is very Wordsworthian — development of the Soul, sort of thing. Let me know if you'd like your name on the front page and hurry up too.

As ever, Bessie.

[75]

P.O.Box 15, Serowe
19 February 1972

Dear Randolph,

I'm going to dedicate a few more books to you so I can receive typed, legible letters!

No, indeed, Paddy Kitchen is still very much a part of my life. She said she and Dulan live a very tempered, even life so she was very interested in people who have nervous breakdowns. I suspect she is looking for some material for a novel. She certainly spends a great deal of time writing in the papers about my books and chose *Maru* as one of the books of the year for 1971.

God knows, I'm working like hell this side to meet the July deadline. The third book lacks the rebounding, rhetorical rhythm of *Maru*... "He wished he could leave the matter with the remark he had passed to Ranko, that the creator of all this vitality was simply a great woman in herself with no other attachments or identification..." I am not writing lines like that. The shaky, jerky hand of the invalid dominates here, but all the same a vividly alive invalid. The arguments are about the soul and again I split myself into the male lead. Look at Makhaya and you have me, at a certain stage of development. Look at *Maru* and you have me — a bounding leap ahead. Someone said there is such a sharp break in the styles of *Rain Clouds* and *Maru* that *Maru* seems to be totally different mind at work. Not so sharply different is the third book from *Maru* except that I haven't the pounding rhythm of it. *Maru* needn't be a treatise on racialism — it can just simply be a symphony of words strung together. But it is both. Here now I am trapped by arguments. The style is flat, prosaic:

What is love?

Who is God?

If I cry, who will have compassion on me as my suffering is the suffering of others?

This is the nature of evil. This is the nature of goodness.

It is the way I attempt to answer these questions that might get the book rejected. So many people here, alarmed by the breakdown assumed a care of my life: "What are you writing now, Bessie?" they ask. I threw out some of the material, mentioning the snags. They said: "Yes, it might be rejected because your arguments are not the conventional ones for goodness and evil, even though they are interesting". I called the book finally after many changes of title — *A Question of Power* — and the key line to it goes something like this ... "if the things of the soul are really a question of power then any one in possession of power of the spirit can be called Lucifer ..." It might not be quite the right way to say it but it is one of the last lines in the book from which I take the title. It is there at the back of my mind and I might like to shape it in another way. I have this feeling about a lot of lines right through — they ought to be shaped and re-shaped. The real truth is a conflict of mind/feeling. There is on the one hand an experience of catatonic shock, the extreme state where the ego has been violently destroyed. No one can live without an ego. So what I really lived through was death in life. On the other the joy of living again is so intense that I totally lack humility. It isn't that I err to the point of arrogance but I am anxious to re-capture a state so low and to pin point it basically as a great achievement. Within the terms of my argument I was driven to such extremes where no one loved anyone. They were barking savagely all the time. They were neither animal, human or anything but permanently growling hideous, savage beasts. When I bust up I simply howled. The torrent of hatred was hitting me blow by blow with a wild panting hysteria — die, die, die, die, you dog, oh you dog, I hate you, I hate you, I hate you. Illogically I ran out of the house shouting at people, shouting at anyone who approached me. That's why I was locked up. I had no way of breaking the storm of evil, it had totally overwhelmed me after four years of silent endurance.

Then you question why? Why did the forces of hell choose me for an experiment in total destruction. You hit an abyss where people's prayers are a mockery. But the Afrikaner Boer, the Klu Klux Klan are a reality there. You have to look at wild, savage evil, relentless, merciless cruelty, then you understand them and they are only a small summary of a terrible darkness of the soul.

When people pray: "Oh God, help me," they are praying to

160

something the have in their minds that is consistently tender, a concept of goodness that is almost feminine in its supposed pity and mercy. Then they walk around generally looking like this God they are praying to — because when I came out of the loony bin I stared hard a people's faces with an almost blank detachment of heart and I saw there a softness and vague un-plannedness, a helplessness, a childlike pity and appeal. I saw it because those were the people I shouted at and shook so hard in the vehement flaying of the fight to break free from hell that a few of them nearly died alongside of me. One woman burst into tears. She said: "The day you broke down I broke down alongside you. I only remained out of bed but I broke too."

Then I thought: "They are praying to a God they will never see because there is no God like ordinary people. There is no one in heaven or hell with ordinary human kindness and decency. I know because I came face to face with strutting bastards who had been Mary Magdalene and all kinds of shit to mankind and she was just a pissing pervert. And there was another bastard who claimed to be the director of the universe and he was a drop lower than Mary Magdalene in his capacity to just shoot out a long stream of piss. Mind you, he so awed himself because he could command angels in the sky to sing: "GLORY BE TO GOD ON HIGH AND ON EARTH PEACE TO MANKIND." That was the sort of hell I lived with, a long yelling, screaming nightmare. It just came. It was there, a part and parcel of Botswana where they get prophecies about God.

I wasn't destined to survive. I wasn't supposed to be alive after 1971 onwards. A coffin was right there. I was buried. I was stone dead and done for and so ill that life was a hazy nightmare of eternal darkness. Between that and death something happened, so suddenly, I don't know what turned the tide back to life. I had a sensation of being lifted and flung bodily right back again, like a big jump over a space into territory when everything was peaceful and resolved. Like a mighty Hercules I raised my arms and snapped link after link of the chains of hell and then swung around like a king Canute before the ocean of creative genius. Like Canute I had to put out my hands to push back the ocean. I hadn't the physical strength but from it I could see that all people are fed, all people are loved.

Hell is like this. I have power and exquisite sensations. I'll give you a little to eat you dog. I'll put my mouth on the spring of your life and suck it dry because I am really the most important person around here. Now dog, get down to the level I dictate to you. You are inferior. You are filth. I hate you, but ah, I need a dog to lap up a little bit of the exquisite sensation I dish out now and then. I only need dogs around here and you are my chief dog. Crawl, bitch!

That was my learning. It was not beautiful.

Bessie

[76]

P.O. Box 15, Serowe
4 June 1972

Dear Randolph,

I am weeping and weeping this side. My third book was rejected by Gollancz. I did take rejection into account but not the way they did it, just dumped it hastily back to my agent with no proper explanation. Now Hilary Rubinstein, my agent, first wrote to me saying that the book was unprintable. Due to this, he said he was not going to post it on to my American publishers. He had no right to do that because I am under contract to show my American publishers my third book and they might give me pointers as to why it is so unprintable, and sympathetic help. The book has been circulated right round Swaneng and everyone loved it. I handed my typescript on to anyone who wanted to read it and received many helpful and glowing comments. I haven't lived in a situation like this before where there are so many who like reading and it has been eagerly snatched from hand to hand. No one jumped up the wall about loony or anything like that but a lot of people cried.

Hilary Rubinstein has me tearing my hair out. He is rushing to suppress the book. I wrote him a furious letter and asked him to hand one of the typescripts to Paddy Kitchen and one to Kenneth Mackenzie and his wife Myrna. I worked with Ken Mackenzie on *Drum* in Cape Town and he and his wife wrote to me. I just wanted to get the typescripts away from Hilary as he is so frightened by the book he just wants it scrapped. He is forcing me to find a new agent and the row blew up so suddenly I haven't collected my wits. I am more depending on Ken Mackenzie to come up with something than Paddy and I would very much like you to eventually get the copy I told Hilary to give to Paddy. I was not sure you would be in London so I asked Paddy to take the copy away from Hilary Rubinstein. I was forced to write behind his back to my American publishers and report that he had refused to transfer the typescript, to them. The Americans, McCalls, who brought out *Maru* as well, have had their names changed to Saturday Review Press. *Maru* was given such a terrific welcome there that they asked a fellow traveller this way to look me up. She came over Easter and saw me parcelling up the typescripts to Hilary and Gollancz. She wrote to the Saturday Review Press saying she had met me and that I had a book on the way. They then wrote asking for the book and my letter to them about Hilary crossed in the post. So I might still get a sympathetic and helpful approach from them. I enclose all the correspondence about this matter for you to see. I am still waiting to hear from all concerned, but my heart is very unsettled by the quarrel with Hilary.

Could you let me know when you would be in London so that I can ask Paddy Kitchen to arrange transfer of the typescript she has, to you?

I have a friend in New York to whom I always send copies of anything I write so I asked her to loan her copy of my book to Saturday Review Press.

As ever,
Bessie.

P.S. The same thing happened to my mother. She was locked up in a loony bin to save the family name.

[77]

P.O. Box 15, Serowe
21 July 1972

Dear Randolph,

Thank you for your letter of June 13th. By the time you receive this letter my typescript will most probably be with James Currey. I have just written to Paddy asking her to pass it on to him. You must have links with James Currey. Didn't we all work together on the *New African*? I remember his name so well and his face but not the surroundings in which I talked to him in Cape Town. He's at Heinemann's. He wrote me a short cover note with the Heinemann edition of *Maru*. I just took it into my head to ask him to go through *A Question of Power* for me. Could you get in touch with

James Currey and make some arrangements about getting the typescript? I keep on expecting a rejection and my final plan was in any case to give you the carbon typescript for your own keeping since it seems unlikely that it would be accepted anywhere. The subject makes people react very emotionally to the book, each one putting up his own particular performance.

Gollancz produced a terrific performance from Naomi Mitchison. They usually hand her my typescripts to vet for libel. I'm black, you see and likely to say dirty things about people. You can't trust black. Well, this time she gave them the Botswana lowdown, indeed. Why, she knew every bloody character in the book! She wrote me quite a hysterical letter, titillated beyond words and demanding to know why I had not made Seretse *real*. This frustrated her. She wanted the book re-written with Seretse *real*.

There is no titillating gossip in the book. It is stark, bleak tragedy from beginning to end. It is written at two levels. The everyday level involves a development project. The people I work with come in and keep moving steadily and sanely through the book, just as beautiful as they are in real life. The second level is a journey inwards into the soul, with three soul characters, who are really disembodied persons, the concentration is on arguments of power, good and evil and it is really in the form of dream sequences which had a thread of logic, the sort of logic of war. This section is so terrible that indeed it would be impossible for living human beings to carry on like that, except in Hitler's Germany, where they did indulge in horrific cruelties and perversions.

The only person who caught the two levels at which the book was written was Ken Mackenzie. He wrote me a beautiful letter saying that this book is the best thing I've ever written. I asked Ken to transfer the copy he has on to

McCalls as they do not really have a copy to work on if they are interested in the book. So you could check with either Paddy or James Currey for the carbon I asked Hilary to give Paddy.

The next thing is I wrote to Hilary Rubinstein. I no longer have a London agent. I told Hilary that I am damn well, bloody well not working with him any more. I told him he is a money grabber who watches the cash till and does not care a damn about the struggle I might have been through to record my own learning ... He wrote me awful, patronising letters. I told him another agent would collect my things and asked Ken/Paddy to fix me up with a new agent.

Ken says it is a big, beautiful book, should find a publisher and attract wide attention when it came out. He said it filled him with wonder. The soul parts are a valuable, detailed record of a mind under intolerable strain and he has not read of anything like that before.

As ever,
Bessie

[78]

P.O. Box 15, Serowe
16 August 1972

Dear Randolph,

I've just had news that James Currey wants Heinemann's to take the book. You know he is in their African dept. He has transferred the typescript to the general fiction section of Heinemann's so that the contract is first made in hardcover. James will later bring it out in the African series of Heinemann's. The copy James Currey had came from Paddy Kitchen. I thought James Currey would reject it too so I asked him on rejection, to hand it on to you. To my surprise, he adores it. The copy which Hilary Rubinstein handed to Ken Mackenzie was later posted by Ken to my American publishers. I have no word from them but will let you know, soon.

Hilary Rubinstein is *no longer* my agent. I have a new one, Giles Gordon, my former Gollancz editor. He wrote asking for my work and I accepted because he is familiar with my style and preoccupations.

Hold on a minute. You will soon see the book and the dedication. James really likes it.

Will write again soon.
                    Much love,
                    Bessie
Howard is fine. Yes, he appears a lot in the new book.

[79]

P.O. Box 15, Serowe
31 August 1972

Dear Randolph,

You seem to have had a wonderful holiday. How is it that France has baking sun? I heard over the news that it rained all summer in England.

I have just received a very inconclusive letter from James Currey about the book. It looks like he came up against opposition. James did not make clear where the typescript is just now but I had told him, on final rejection, to hand it over to you. If you receive it at some stage later and want to hand it on to Collins, please contact my agent, Giles Gordon.

His address is: Giles Gordon, Anthony Sheil Associates Ltd, 52 Floral Street, London WC2 9DA.

Giles Gordon is an acquaintance of Ken Mackenzie and Ken says he is a very friendly man. Giles was my Gollancz editor. He rejected *Power*. Then resigned from Gollancz. I left Hilary at the time and he asked to be my agent, much to my surprise because he said horrible things about the book. In any case, we had a correspondence going for two years as he edited *Maru* and he became somewhat interested in my refugee life and tried to get me a passport, but he dropped the idea when I went to the loony bin. He does not come over so clearly in his letters. They are terribly stiff and formal and he seems very upper class and snotty. In any case you are somewhat upper class too but not snotty. You might like him.

I have not yet had a final decision from my American publishers but I will let you know.

I'll just make a few footnotes to the book *Power*. I have a great character there, Sello. Very similar to Maru but with greater projection of thought, torture and control. The superficial reader would not grasp the power behind the man. It is argued out — the man's perfection at the heights is based on what he did in his depths of degradation. Pasternak says: "I could never love anyone who had not fallen or stumbled ..." and this bears out my own argument for my character. Small, piddling goodness is not for me. Oh, of course one could produce a book about a church mouse but my name will never be there. Again, on the surface obscene things are mentioned but the writer is not dedicated to obscenity. It is a part of learning about what goes on in hell. So there is a blending, of everything and in the end you get a huge hotch potch like a Van Gogh painting or as you like to say, a sprawling run across the universe taking in everything.

I'll write again as soon as I hear from America.

The blessed garden work takes up all my time and I have

to plan the next book in between planting cabbages, then type till two a.m. in the morning.

One of these days old age will catch up with me.

As ever,
Bessie

[80]

P.O. Box 15, Serowe
29 October 1972

Dear Randolph,

A letter you wrote me on the 27th Sept., has just arrived. It was diverted to surface mail because it had no postage. I have also received your letter of 20th October.

Giles wrote to me saying he had met you. There are two copies of *Power* in America and he is getting one back and he told me he would let you read it before keeping it in his office for business purposes. He's really a damn good agent. I could not have put my affairs in more efficient hands and there is a billion dollar business relationship building up between him and me if I can get my books written. *Power*, anyway, was the sort of book everyone who read it, reacted to. He swung round, unpredictably to friendship. Other people read the book and abruptly broke off the friendship. The "snotty and upper class" I referred to comes out of the sort of complicated undertone English people add to their relationships with people. This writing business has so many confidences — a writer confides more out of the way things than other people might and no one really remains impersonal and unknown. A sort of acquaintance with an English man or woman is like striking up a friendship with a rabbit. They never say what they mean, like if I like you I say I like you and you can feel secure about it. They say under pressure that they don't like you but they mean they like you. Can you understand that? Often I have found that things go smoothly between Giles and me and suddenly something sets him off like an explosion. I've learnt to tab the sorts of things likely to upset him and bypass them because suddenly in all the formality he'll break out into a very personal outburst, usually something to do with not liking me at that particular period and I can be told off in a very sharp manner. It is all incomprehensible to me except that I sense how to avoid the outbursts. If you think perhaps your paths might cross, simply through your getting involved in my affairs, it might take you a whole year to understand and like Giles. The surface part of him is so good — he keeps his promises. He takes note of every detail missing nothing as far as work goes.

James' might have told you that I have started re-writing *Power* with Richard Lister. Re-writing to tidy it up. Lister has a control over the story only Ken and his wife had and immediately got the point of it — he said... "it is a prolonged spiritual crisis, seen from the inside and powerfully described ..." Please tell me when Giles hands you the carbon of *Power*. I shall send you the re-written pages which you can insert for me, in that copy.

Pat van Rensburg told me you had been involved in an effort with Canon Collins to raise some money for me. Thank you very much. I have worked for Pat's project for two years on a voluntary basis as I had money from my books. I ran out of it this year and he is paying me ten pounds a month till I get on my feet again. I have agreed with Giles to do a profile — one of these "around-the-world" series — on village life in Serowe. Pantheon books in America requested it but I doubt they will give me an advance until I produce the typescript. It is easy enough work to get through and after that I wanted to try a biography on a certain chief named, Khama the Great. I stumbled on to details of his life while looking for material to send Ken about his great grand-dad, John Mackenzie. Khama is an extremely interesting personality and everything, the tone and feel of the country, are overshadowed by him — the sort of complicated, fluid, flexible hero of my other books but I think more confined to a power structure than interests me. I have worked out my philosophies, anti-power, anti-social and never bothered to examine what it means to have a fluid, unbending personality within a power structure, to use power for one's own ends and others.

As ever, Bessie

P.S. Sorry to hear about the illness of Betty Sleath. Please give her my love. Yes, refer to Caroline's offer later.

[81]

P.O. Box 15, Serowe
29 December 1972

Dear Randolph,

Thank you for your greetings. *Power* is in the clear. An unexpected offer was made for it by a totally new publisher, Davis-Poynter. He's just come in but he used to be managing director for McGee and resigned to go into publishing on his own. He has only published a few books so far. I hear from my agent that he had been sitting on the novel when suddenly and unexpectedly an article appeared about me in the *Guardian*. It was an overnight decision based on the article which tallied with what he had read in the book. The journalist interviewed me some months ago so I was as surprised as Giles by the offer. At first I did not even get the firm's name, Giles wrote me a very excited offer. They made a big joke about the *Guardian* piece because Davis-Poynter accused Giles of putting it there especially to push him into buying the book and Giles was quite stunned because he had no idea about it. Nor did I because I forgot the interview.

I have just heard from Davis-Poynter himself. He says he likes the book ... "it is a most distinguished novel ..." He and James are teaming up.

Pat left last week for a month's holiday at the holiday resort in Northern Botswana.

Howard had a very bad school report this year. He failed all his tests and is right at the bottom of the class. To follow on this, I was told a joke about a small boy in England. It is entitled:

WILL YOU HAVE SOME MORE TEA, VICAR?

A small boy was fond of swearing. One day his mother called him aside and said:

"You must not swear today. The vicar is coming to tea. You know you always wanted a wheel-barrow and if you don't swear while the Vicar is here, we'll buy you a wheel-barrow."

On the arrival of the Vicar, they all sat down to tea. There were trifles and cake for tea. The mother said:

"Would you have some trifle, Vicar?"

"No thank you," the Vicar replied, faintly. "I never touch it."

"Then would you have some cake, Vicar?"

"No thanks," the Vicar said. "I never eat cake."

In the meanwhile the small boy had been listening and glowering. Suddenly he said: "Give the bugger a boiled egg and to hell with the wheel-barrow."

In the embarrassed silence that followed, his mother said: "Would you like some more tea, Vicar?"

As ever,
Bessie.

[82]

P.O. Box 15, Serowe

24 February 1973

Dear Randolph,

Thank you for the *Times* article on my new publisher. He looks very impressive.

My new book is due in six months' time, with the dedication. It is also dedicated to Ken and Myrna Mackenzie — so you will look out won't you?

I guess you are very busy just right now; so I won't write a long letter. Things are fine here. In case they go seriously wrong, (I don't feel secure), Ken and Myrna are going to legally adopt Howard. They agreed and we are busy with lawyers. Do you know the whereabouts of Harold?

Much love,
Bessie.

[83]

P.O. Box 15, Serowe

6 April 1973

Dear Randolph,

I've just come from Pat's house. He's away in Sweden just now but he returns on Tuesday 10th. His wife leaves on the 12th for England for a course in weaving, for a year. She said there is indeed a mix-up about the money you sent but Pat will sort it out on his arrival. I gave her your message.

Yes, tell your friends who want to visit Botswana that there is a safari hotel in the Chobe Game Reserve in the North West of Botswana, which is there for tourists who want to see the wild game. They will get more details from Botswana airways which run a flight there on their arrival. It's better to visit in the cooler months, the summers are no joy at all; either drought or terrible downpours and lightning storms, and deadening heat. The cool months are from May to mid-August. The North West is malaria area so people going there have to take a tablet every day. It is also infested with tsetse fly. I don't know how the Botswana govt. gets around this in their tourist propaganda but apparently mankind will go anywhere.

Naomi never loved me. The events of the breakdown, the letter I handed to her at the time rather cooled things off. Her world trained her to cope with decent problems and dinner was always on time. She came around here but shut her mouth up about the book. She was scared I'd make a scene but then I can't quarrel with an old lady who might die any time and I was amused to see just how scared she is of scenes. I come from a rough world where scenes are a part of the day's work. In between she let me know that she is convinced that I am insane but she thinks Howard is a balanced child and would like to invite him to her mansion in Scotland. Not so his mother. But she has used her life constructively.

About the Carvlin man. He became too emotionally involved in my affairs. It frightened him and he pulled out of the correspondence but what a man he is! I never cared to bother him. Friends come and go for strange reasons.

I'd be pleased to have news of Harold. He last wrote to me from the McDougall colony in US, a philanthropic settlement for writers going through lean times. I read about the colony in a magazine. Harold wrote when *Maru* came out, that was about two years ago. I simply want a divorce but I will only pursue the matter if someone wants to marry me. So far there is no sign of such a happening. Indeed I never bothered. I was going through such hell that I hardly seemed to be a human being anymore. Then I went and aged dramatically beyond my years. I just have grey hairs and an early menopause. Some people are like that, life treats them so unusually they do everything beforehand.

The Davis-Poynter man knows that *A Question of Power* is trouble. More likely to raise a mocking jeer. No other publisher would touch it. But James Currey seems to take it in dead earnest. It was James who held on to it for a long time when no one wanted it. I've never had it so bad before. In this business a lot of favourable opinions count but the material of the book gives no choice. It is so desperate. James must have told you why he hung on to the book. For myself, unlike Faust, I did not really offer my soul to the devil. I simply had to observe his values. You can't often do that unless you get quite close and make like buddy-buddy. But Satan is a ghastly sight.

Much love,
Bessie

I have United Nations travel documents for Howard and me and can leave anytime but as yet I haven't enough money.

[84]

P.O. Box 15, Serowe
30 May 1973

Dear Randolph,

I say this with heavy sarcasm. I suppose you can ask me important questions on postcards? I suppose you can solve philosophical riddles on post cards?

A Question of Power is taken from a key line in my book

— "If the things of the soul are really a question of power, then anyone in possession of power of the Spirit could be Lucifer ..."

God, I'm depressed. Penguin half commissioned a book from me, made me work like hell on research night after night then turned snotty about my material. It's called: *Serowe: The Village of the Rain Wind*. After 29,000 words, they say they want to ditch me because I won't co-operate with their style and write what they want. I mean there's limits. I have to produce the bloody book. What a waste of time!

Much love,
Bess

[85]

P.O. Box 15, Serowe
23 September 1973

Dear Randolph,

I'd feel very hurt if you had to actually buy a copy of *A Question of Power*. I am arranging for my publishers to send you a copy on my account as the book is dedicated to you. I enclose a copy of my letter to my publishers asking them to send you and Ken and Myrna a copy each of the book.

A lot is on the go. First Davis-Poynter like and admire *Power* so much they have entered it and only it of their lists for the Booker prize. The winner will be announced on November 28th and if I should win, I'll fly over to London. I have United Nations travel documents for Howard and me. The judges this year are Mary McCarthy, Edna O'Brien and Karl Miller. So pending luck I might see you by Christmas. I wish I could win it just to simplify my life a bit and find a country to stay in. I can't die leaving Howard a stateless person and I believe the prize money is quite high — forty thousand pounds.

It would be a bit of a wrench to leave because I have such a grasp of our way of life here and it could never be as perfect anywhere else. This is just what I am busy with at present, my fourth, non-fiction book — *Serowe: The Village of the Rain Wind*. The village was founded in 1902 by Khama the Great. Amazingly, I lived here for nine years unaware of Khama and I was forced to do some research for Ken and Myrna about their grand-dad, John Mackenzie. Actually the missionaries wrote little on him but volumes on Khama whom they all worshipped and that is how I banged into the gentleman, quite by accident. I looked at the old man this way and that and fell violently in love with him. He is a classic, all by himself, the lofty God of Mount Olympus, the great Lincoln of Southern Africa. Tshekedi Khama was his son.

I have divided my *Serowe* book into three sections — The Era of Khama the Great; The Era of Tshekedi Khama and lastly the Swaneng Project. The theme is one of social reform and educational advance and people tell it to me in their own words. I link story to story with a slight historical narrative. Everyone agrees with me that Serowe is the greatest village in Africa, so I am just making this clear to everyone else. It's a very beautiful book, even if I the author have to say so and though it shows how people work and plough during the different eras, it isn't boring at all — at least I like it very much. I am actually mid-way and have about 30,000 words to go. I doubt I'll be through if I have to come to London in November or December. But I hope to bring it with me, take a month's holiday there and correct the typescript with whoever is my publishers. Actually Penguin commissioned it then got mad as hell because I wouldn't give up the original plan to weave the book around Khama, Tshekedi and the

Swaneng work. They said I couldn't go around saying there were great men here. The bloody cheek of them! I sold Giles Gordon thoroughly on the idea of the book and he said I should just get right on with it my way and he'll fix the publisher. You must know much more about Tshekedi and Pat's work but everything started with Khama. If I win that prize I'll set me down for three years on his biography, not only him but the complete understanding of Southern Africa, just what went wrong and how people lost the land.

I am pissed off with the shitty politics of this country that is why I want to leave. There is an unhappy sense that it isn't right. Apart from lots of anguish I have endured here.

As ever,
Bess

P.S. Please type out your comments on *Power* so I can read it.

[86]

P.O. Box 15, Serowe
28 November 1973

Dear Randolph,

Your letter was totally illegible, of course, and I could not make out a word, so don't forget to type the next one.

I am scrawling this very hastily at the post office just to show I'm alive.

Pat Cullinan wants to come and see me. I am dithering in agony about plans to leave here. I was out of touch with the Cullinans for years, then he heard indirectly I'd been in the loony bin and was alarmed out of his mind. I sent him the book. He'll more or less help me to plan things. A lot is not right here and we have no hope of citizenship.

Did you recognise Pat van Rensburg in *Power* as the "Eugene man"? Howard is so well and very busy with "boy's things" — football, cowboy films etc; school work is always an afterthought with him!

Much love,
Bess

[87]

P.O. Box 15, Serowe
9 December 1973

Dear Randolph,

This letter will be posted in London by a young teacher who is leaving Swaneng on holiday.

I had a good laugh at your psychological "fixing" of the Penguin lady. Someone else at Penguin, James Price, gave me hell for half a year. Penguin commissioned the *Serowe* book I'm working on at present and asked for a synopsis. When I produced the synopsis, James Price produced a counter synopsis — he wanted me to work on a very loose frame and I had fixed up a very tight frame of work, outside of which I could introduce anything of interest. I refused to give up my synopsis and they threw me out bodily and said they never wanted to see my stuff again; it was too ambitious. I'll really collapse if they want the *Power* book.

I have done a little work, very little, in my *Serowe* book, on Khama the Great. The real work, if I ever attempt it, is still far in the future. No doubt I haven't got him in focus at all — my own complicated needs dominate just now and no doubt my own needs go into all I write about Khama at present and I have used all my material at hand on an entirely intuitive basis, interpretations of compassion in social reform, compassion towards refugees and his personal power in leadership which was a strong factor with the invading whites — they all duly noted that powerful dignity he carried around with him.

I'd tentatively decided that if I stay here, I'd write a novel, fitting him into the context of Southern Africa at that time. If so, that novel would be scaled down to his village involvement and worked out at the level of him and his people and where he was carrying them. Khama has the drama of a man who goes against the grain and he is a rare species indeed. If I leave Botswana by June, I shall have to re-organise my whole life and writing. I might attempt that "cold, detached" biography as the material is available in the British Museum anyway. It would be easier to do research in London. But I am not so established as a writer to have people falling over their feet to help me and once I leave here I might not be able to earn my living as a writer. My income is very unpredictable and I am only just beginning to get a control. I am experienced enough with publishers to know how hard is the game they play and to a certain extent I have benefitted from hard terms, so that I knock up the best I can so far. It doesn't really matter here if I haven't money for a stretch of six months or so but it would matter in England and America where life is much more complicated.

One thing that interests me about Khama is the question of natural genius or intelligence, *without book learning*. I have seen how it works out in village life as I have worked with completely illiterate people who are brilliant at picking up facts and details and he had that knack. Wherever there is that kind of spark, you get records of it and the missionaries and travellers wrote reams about Khama. There are some men who did little but live accurately and people love this. I don't know how I gave the impression of being attracted to

Khama in the first place if the feeling had not been broadly justified. Do you know much of Randolph Churchill, the son of Churchill? There is nothing of his father's greatness in him and there is nothing of the Khama magic left really in the present generation of Khamas. They seem gifted with one quality only, a belief that they are royalty but a lot of them are very rich and selfish. There is a terrible sense of "absence" in Seretse Khama who is the president of Botswana and he is in practical reality famous for making the most inane, insipid political speeches — "he never did a foolish thing and he never said a wise one.".

As time goes on one begins to get a fatal sense that one does not understand African politics and that the whole process of liberation is very destructive, not to whites, they always have money and careers, but to blacks. They asked the young man Tom, of my *Power* book, to leave the country in 14 days' time. No one understands that sinister gesture. It is just something in the air and he wasn't so dramatic as a revolutionary. Most of those letters — leave the country in 14 days —have been sent to South African refugees and few had anywhere to go except back to South Africa. In that context, as a refugee I must identify with the people who have been deported and realise that there is no place for me.

I keep on setting June 1974 as my deadline for leaving Botswana but the struggle I have put up for survival here has been so prolonged and bitter and dangerous, it is as though a huge chunk of my life has been hammered out of me by forces that I will never comprehend, except that they are terribly evil and destructive.

Pat Cullinan has just written to say that he will come to see me in February or March. I accepted because I thought I could talk out the practical details with him on where do I go, what do I do and how do I start life all over again in some other country. I don't have much resources, emotional resources left — one can see the limits to which an individual can help himself. And yet at the back of my mind I am aware of tremendous reserves of strength and discipline I never had when I was younger. I think I only dread the insecurity of a new choice but for Howard's sake I'll have to make it. It's possible that if I leave here I can live to a good old age and bring him up and educate him.

I am just deeply sorry I ever came to Botswana and learnt all I have here about human sorrow and evil. And yet I might have had to work it all out here. The suffering was so intensely lonely that people insist that I made it up all on my own. All that is left for me to do is pack up my bags and leave. Ten years of my life are almost unaccounted for, except through those three books. I did propose individual loneliness, but was actually unprepared to accept it for a long time. Most people live uncomplicated lives. They have work and quietly rear their children. There is an order and sanity about them that keeps the world going. There is an outer disorder and insanity about my life which makes me a victim. One of the disorders is that they won't give us citizenship here, they just won't and I think they use refugees as political pawns in the Southern African context — we are a small crowd but it pleases the South Africans and Rhodesians when we are not accepted here. I've come to see that it isn't a hoax but a real cruelty. The second thing is my awareness of evil and a clear vision of direct interference in my life from an outside source. Put both problems together and they overwhelm me. It's always a big thing with me — if I am working something out, it's not only for myself, it's going to help others as well. I only find that my health isn't strong enough for battle here any more. I can't go on living under these conditions which offer nothing but suffering. Most times the only person who makes any human gesture is Pat Van Rensburg and then in a limited way and indeed, there is a tremendous amount of work to do here but it's not a happy life.

Much love,
Bessie

[88]

P.O. Box 15, Serowe
17 April 1974

Dear Randolph,

You don't have to describe the heather. I might be seeing it for myself one of these days.

Some one is arranging for me to apply for Norwegian citizenship. It is a long way to go to become a citizen of a country but it is the only really secure offer I have had. Things are not final yet as some papers of mine are being presented to the committees there. But the arrangement is that I should come over in July or August.

I would stop over in London for about two weeks in July or August only if *my Serowe book were accepted* and I could work on the copy editing. Otherwise I shall proceed straight to Norway with Howard. I am a little worried about what is going to happen to him education wise as I don't know how he will manage with the language and it might turn out that I would have to send him to school in England, while I sit out the 5 to 7 years trying to acquire citizenship. I'll be something like 42 before I am a citizen of any country and ten years went by here with no hope of it really.

Now, if I am still alive after 42 and have a best-seller behind me, I am going to take a slow boat around the world and see the rubber trees in Brazil, the temples in India, etc, etc — in fact the whole world. I'll send you a post card right from the top of the Himalayas, whence I shall be transported in a special helicopter, because I'll be so famous!! ha,ha.

But getting back to Howard's education. Would you advise boarding school for him in England and a fairly sane one. I believe the boarding schools there are snobbish and teach the children bad values. He can manage very well with English but I am afraid that he would not be able to cope, school-wise, with Norwegian and he is able to enter high school, just now. He's 12 on May 15th. I know he'd have to learn French, but it wouldn't be the medium of instruction, like Norwegian would. I think it would be too much for him to catch up with school instruction in Norwegian — that's the main draw back. I'd been asked to let him into the school there because his education would then be *free right through to university*, but it might take him three or four to five years to learn the language alone. I am supposed to learn it during a re-orientation course which lasts for about 18 months and he might be able to get a citizenship through me while he is five years out of the country on studies, say in England. What do you think of this? What school could you suggest? Also I might get a job in advance before I get there to help with the fees.

Suggest a school where they treat black children decently and everything is okay. He'd do very well in the English medium instruction, as he's been getting here but I thought the Norwegian medium might throw him right off course and be more than he could cope with. I was told that there was an English medium school in Oslo but the person arranging things for me did not know any details about it. I could always get him for the holidays and I shall be right away issued with Norwegian travel documents. If I have to stop over in London July or August I could arrange about

Howard's school — it would have to be a boarding school — so could you suggest what could be done? Please type the reply as I cannot read your handwriting very well and you might have some suggestions about a school.

As ever,
Bessie

Send me some idea of boarding school fees for 1 year.

[89]

P.O. Box 15, Serowe
12 May 1974

Dear Randolph,

I'll start off my letter by saying that I'm not going to Norway, after all. I'd been working at terrible speed to meet the deadline Giles had set so we could work out whether I needed to stop over in London for the copy editing on the Serowe book before proceeding to Norway. I made the deadline of April 30th but then I had to read the book through before posting it and that finally finished me up. It is a damn beautiful book and I simply thought: "After work like that with so much humour, value and information, this is my home, and only death will take me out of it." So I set my focus straight a bit, if one can call my reasoning straight. There's nothing but death for me so I might as well get busy on a few more books. Howard will be 17 in five years time and I might be around still to see him get that big. For now I have given him a very secure childhood. He's never had to worry about anything and after that he'll have to fight his own battles about citizenship or anything else he needs. No one ever protected me and I've been through real hell and right until I die, I'm likely to be all alone. If life is that grim for me, he can take a little of it too. We couldn't help what happened

185

here. We could not have known what the government would do to refugees, so it is something outside our control. What I can control is the peace and order of my life here. And it's a beautiful environment for a child to grow up in. Howard is so completely a person of this country in ways and thoughts — he came here when he could barely walk and he looks very critically at everything I do. "You don't do the right thing," he said to me one day. "It's important to know people's names and you must not just say Dumela Mma and Dumela Rra. That's all you know."

If all goes well he could get some of his education here, then I'll see. They may say they don't want any of the children of refugees in the schools because last year they took down his name. If so, we can see what can be worked out about getting him out of here. I only expect evil to come out of my decision because there is evil in the country but then I have experienced so much of it that whatever happens next cannot destroy my life any more than it has been destroyed already. That side of the story can run its own course. If all goes well I'll type out a few more books.

You know, publishers skin you to death. Giles says Davis-Poynter is having a hard time selling *A Question of Power* and they're not giving me any more money until I cover the advance they gave me. But the buggers eat on the expense account of the cash they draw in from our work. They wouldn't exist without writers and when I say I haven't a bloody cent in my purse, they say they don't just give away money. So I don't think I'd ever get to London or anything like that simply because I'll never have the money.

This is only the courage of death that's left to me. That's all I have left Randolph. There's nothing else. But it makes me feel peaceful at last.

As ever,
Bessie

186

[90]

P.O. Box 15, Serowe
26 August 1974

Dear Randolph,

Thank you for the review. Yes, I've had Ronald Blythe here in book form, for over a year now. He is the author of *Akenfield: Portrait of an English Village* and I had to pattern *Serowe: Village of the Rainwind* on his work. Yes most reviews were like his, they were forced to say the book — *A Question of Power* is "magnificent" but they all took a dodge behind this "mentally sick" business. It often gives the effect that they have mis-read the book mainly because the language is too embarrassing to handle; it hardly sounds normal or human; it's not easy to shuttle or argue with, so they tried to re-set the book in South Africa because this sort of thing ... "there's strange under-currents and events here ..." could not apply to Botswana. They dare not examine such language as ... "I thought too much of myself. I am the root cause of human suffering ..."

I am still tied to the *Serowe* book and it has hardly moved off the ground mainly because my publishers were on holiday. It looks like everything closes down there for the summer and people work like hell during the winter! Betty Sleath will eventually know the date of publication of the *Serowe* book — it has been accepted so far by Davis-Poynter. She wants to help in its promotion and I am sending a note to Davis-Poynter about this.

I think I told you that I had decided to stay in Botswana, come what may. I really belong here in spite of refugee status and other things, so I'll see what happens. God, this is a terribly unhappy time to be alive. Everything is so uncertain.

I had a spill-over of material from the Serowe book and at present I am trying to work this into a small collection of short stories, which James Currey said he might take for the African Writers' Series. It's mainly village tales centred around the breakdown of family life. I'd told Betty Sleath I'd dedicate the small collection to her if James buys it but I've never worked much on short stories and I'm afraid he'll find the work a bit dull and flat.

I keep on toying around with Khama the Great. The man's image haunts me but the work may be beyond me and a waste of time. That's all I have at the back after I am through with *Serowe* and the collection of short stories. When I really think of writing a historical novel, my heart begins to fall to my feet. I'll only go in for it if I can catch hold of a central feeling of magic to keep me going, a vast kind of panorama of tribal life, with Khama as the dominant character. I can't shake the man off. He fascinates me. But unfortunately the work is slow and heavy and the research, forbidding. I can't afford something so risky, a heavy job of research and writing for nearly two years with the terribly precarious income I have. No publisher would sponsor me. I only cover basic sales and expenditure. I am not a best-selling type. Norman Mailer was paid $1,000,000 for a novel he'd not written yet!

Otherwise life goes on peacefully enough. Howard is taking his exams to enter secondary school and he's such a nice boy. He's waking up and thinking and likes to engage me in complicated arguments.

The Portuguese coup has raised hopes very high for changes in southern Africa.

Much love,
Bessie

[91]

Hiya Randolph,

Howard won't collect the stamps but I do. Botswana has a magnificent range of them but the stamp people make them too large for our envelopes most times.

All is well except that I've had a bad financial time which I hope will be over soon but writing-wise it's been a good year for me — two more masterpieces due some time from my pen and Davis-Poynter said he'd like me to stay with his firm (of course he also means I have to produce works of genius *and sell.*) He said he liked me; in the understated British way!

I am almost through with a collection of short stories for James Currey and D-P. The book on Serowe has a snag with my American publishers, Pantheon. They are slow to sign the contract.

Much love to you and family. Christmas greetings.

Bessie

[92]

Dear Randolph,

Post card senders ought only to receive post cards in reply. You know British publishing is collapsing and so are writers. I can't say anything just now because business arrangements constantly fall through. But I'll let you know once *Serowe* works out.

Much love, Bessie

After Bessie's spell in Lobatse mental hospital the old terrors were still there and appear at their most obsessive in her 24 September 1971 letter [71]. On the carbon copy in the Serowe archive she has written, beside the two sentences starting with the reference to "Summer Flowers" in the second paragraph: "Keep that for Janet" and at the foot of paragraph three, which ends the page: "The Buddha of family life, the Buddha of women".

In the one before it she had seemed calm [70]. I had written, on 16 March 1971, not knowing she was having mental treatment in Lobatse and as if all was normal: "Your mirth at my churchgoing intrigues me. It doesn't at all conflict with your view of God". I misquoted "Be still and only believe that I am God" (which she silently corrected) and went on: "'Be still' is what church is about, as is 'that peace which the world cannot give'. Also the Anglican liturgy, which, like you, I was brought up with, is to me a form of worship that has truth and beauty, though it is a human invention. I cannot manage an occasional glimpse as when a fly swims in a teacup. I do see God in people and things — where else can a human look?" [70]

The other letter of the same date [69] she did not send. I wish she had — one must regret that her "please keep a hold on me somewhere" was never said and scarcely half observed as time went on. No 70 must have been a "rewrite" but, uniquely, it is unfinished and unsigned.

Patrick van Rensburg wrote in the same month, August 1971, that Bessie was "free of her previous obsessions", but "acutely aware of all her actions previous to her entering the Mental Hospital and is painfully humiliated and apologetic". Patrick had "involved her in helping with the Boiteko garden, which she loves and which gives her some kind of daily routine to hold on to and which makes her feel genuinely useful". She was certainly not "cured" and "although she talks with horror about the mental hospital we will not be afraid to take her quietly back for another spell of treatment before the whole thing becomes exaggerated. And so we will see-saw along". Naomi Mitchison wrote from Argyllshire that Liz van Rensburg had told her also that Bessie was back and "much better though embarrassingly conscious of what she has done in the past". Naomi had written to tell Bessie that she had "done her biography for one of these encyclopedias". She was off to Botswana soon, but as she wrote "had 37 people staying in and round the house", unconscious, perhaps, of the startling contrast with Bessie's "Rain Clouds" and its two rooms.

In late 1971 and early 1972 she was in high spirits about her writing — film rights, best-seller claims for *Maru*, Gollancz pushing her for her third novel. She had moments of seeing herself as a famous writer — and me as a "homely type" [74]. The "very pretty girl" who had failed to report on me was Jacklyn Cock, now professor of sociology at Witwatersrand University and author of *Maids and Madams* (1980). Bill (now Sir Raymond) and Margaret Hoffenberg were a central part of our Cape Town set, until Bill's banning order in 1968 and their move to England.

By August 1972 Patrick van Rensburg was asking me to intercede with Canon Collins, for Bessie by then had no funds, being unable to find a publisher for the "apparently very controversial" new novel *A Question of Power*. "I know at least one person whose judgement I would usually value who thinks it a fine book and undoubtedly her best", Patrick wrote, adding that he had given her R120, paid R20 to have her garden fenced, and was letting her have R20 per month, all of which he had to recover.

I noticed a new asperity in one or two of her letters to me, partly perhaps as I could offer so little in reply to her philosophising strain. Many of the letters after Lobatse show the replacement of her supposed enemies in Serowe with a new set of hate figures — her publishers and literary agents in London. The cutting I have subjected these letters to and the suppression of some names may spare feelings. Those who recognise themselves should bear in mind my words to Bessie at the time: "You seem to specialise in the great love, followed by the great let-down", and remember that most

191

were later restored to somewhere near their earlier pinnacle.

The tangle of publishers' and agents' relationships with her was hard to unravel, even worse her tax problems, but I felt that was my new role, replacing the life-support system of her bad times. The Penguin reader [87] I cannot recall. My "fixing" consisted of my trying to convince her of the significance of *Power*. Penguin did take on *Rain Clouds* in 1971, but my efforts for *Power* failed, as they did with Picador, although the founding editor, Caroline Lassalle (then De Crespigny), was a friend of Bessie's and mine from Cape Town days. After its brief glory — Davis-Poynter's sole Booker Prize entry and some serious reviews — it was consigned to the African Writers' Series by Heinemann. It remains in print — as an "African writing" item and has not yet found its rightful place in universal literature.

The conception of *Serowe: Village of the Rain Wind* I was slow to rejoice in — or of that part of it about Khama the Great. "You must develop a cold, hard detachment from your subject before you can begin to enjoy the luxury of admiration and musing", I wrote in December 1973.

The quest for another home ended with the apparent draining away of much of her bitterness against her Batswana neighbours. There were revelations in the long letter she wrote to the President of Botswana, Sir Seretse Khama in August 1975, and copied to me. It must be one of the most remarkable he ever received — certainly from a South African refugee explaining the plight of her kind. It ended with a brief account of her own role in the subject matter of *A Question of Power*. Of one of her most self-destructive actions when, in February 1971, she put up a placard in the Serowe post office horribly libelling Sir Seretse with obscene accusations, she wrote that she had used *A Question of Power* "to pull that paper down. I am extremely sorry for it and had no intention of dying with such a crime against my name". She ended "I am just happy the sun rises every day and from then on, life usually plans itself for me. I have no plans of my own". Those paragraphs, with their warm references to Lenyeletse Seretse, are among the keys to *Power*.

The first part of the letter to Seretse was about her

intractable tax problems from the neglected past. Wonderful to relate, she wrote on the top of the carbon copy she sent me: "Nothing ever sorts out Botswana, but this letter straightened out my tax here".

Bessie Head in her front yard, Serowe, April 1976 *[Mary Benson]*

5. Serowe (3)

31 December 1975 - 23 July 1976

[93]

P.O. Box 15, Serowe
31 December 1975

Dear Randolph,

I wonder who is rude about sending post cards. You keep silent for months on end and then scrawl: "Here's the heather in Scotland. What's the news ..." That's no way to communicate with a person.

We'll have to see what Botswana gets soon. The whole of Africa has had rotten luck, leadership-wise, and it would be a pity if Botswana threw up Idi Amin or something worse because it has very nice people. I think the Boers and Rhodesians must have their eyes on this country and are only waiting for stupid leadership to take over, then they do. They most probably have the day marked out somewhere. Smith and Vorster are having constant meetings. They just need an Angolan mess, then they walk in. Rhodesia, the black side, has the same history of massacre of black people by black people.

If you want my news, will you please treat the information I send you with great caution. I am going to let off steam a bit and mention some things I suppressed. I wanted to mention everything because I am hopeful that you could introduce me to a new literary agent in London ...

... Half of the story is explained in copies of letters I have enclosed with this letter. Early in the year Giles Gordon wrote to me and asked if I paid tax to the Botswana government. I was liable to under a double taxation agreement I'd signed with the UK to get my earnings cleared through. I wrote back to Gordon that I'd had to go through the formalities here but when the Botswana govt. sent me a tax return, I in turn wrote them a letter of protest about their treatment of refugees ...

... He kept quiet a bit then all hell broke loose. He presented me with a tax problem that was unsolvable. It cleverly hinted that I was being punished by the UK for not paying tax to the Botswana govt. It hinted at everything and how impossible it was for them to send me any more money. So he kept my earnings in England. I was never to know what the UK tax authorities ever wanted from me. That was Giles Gordon's secret. I wrote letters in an attempt to straighten out what I felt was perhaps a discrepancy in my behaviour ...

... Two of my typescripts are with Davis-Poynter. One is the history of *Serowe* and the second is a collection of short stories entitled roughly *Village Tales*. Davis-Poynter offered Pat Cullinan the southern African paperback rights for *Serowe* because Heinemann's AWS did not want it. He offered Pat Cullinan hardcover rights for the *Village Tales* because James Currey at AWS had made an offer for it and D-P wanted AWS to get into southern Africa with the paperback ...

... Pat Cullinan at first blankly pretended that he didn't understand why I'd turned against Giles Gordon. They had a correspondence. Giles Gordon wrote to Pat Cullinan implying that I'd suddenly gone insane. Would Pat see me and try to restore my sanity? Pat Cullinan agreed with him about my possible insanity and said in effect that he'd come over to Serowe and see me pulling faces and things like that and maybe walking around without my clothes on. He'd reassure Giles Gordon. He actually showed me these letters, presumably because I would not mind a discussion on my sanity as I was a self-confessed lunatic.

I showed Pat Cullinan the whole backlog of correspondence. He was in a turmoil ...

... I could only make simple decisions. Davis-Poynter indicated in one letter that he might not make an offer for the *Village Tales*. I can't offer them to James Currey directly because he works through hardcover, but AWS wanted them. Poor as I am I am going to take my work back and not offer it to Pat Cullinan. He frightened me. So you see the mess????

Much love,
Bessie

[94]

P.O. Box 15, Serowe
18 February 1976

Dear Randolph,

Your letter of 5th Feb. heartened me greatly, especially that you had talked to James Currey. Up till now I could get no response out of Davis-Poynter, even though I sent him a cable two weeks ago, out of fear that he might have written and the letter was simply retarded by the censors. This often happens with my mail.

Let me answer your question first:

1. The position with the *Serowe* book is that it ought to be in galleys at Davis-Poynter's just right now. Until June, last year, I had worked with Davis-Poynter on the copy editing. An artist, Polly Loxton, was then involved. She was illustrating the

Serowe book and the last job I had to do was to okay her drawings which she had done from a set of rough photographs I had sent her of life in *Serowe*, and the Botswana section of the British Museum. So, from the artist, who had contact with Davis-Poynter and from my panic-stricken literary agencies, I understood that *Serowe* had gone into galleys. The book had many contributors and one contributor rang up Davis-Poynter requesting that an acknowledgement be inserted. He asked her to come for an interview, which she refused to do saying that she preferred to do it through me but had phoned to ask if it was too late to insert the acknowledgement. He replied that there was time as the book was only in galleys. I am afraid I am a bit panic-stricken as something has gone wrong; I cannot account for the silence. God knows, the commotion with Giles Gordon was VERY bad. I think from your letter, I'll try to find out from James Currey what is what and hope to move things forward. James Currey would be the best person to contact under the circumstances as he was involved in *Botswana Village Tales*, which Davis-Poynter is also holding ...

... I am so relieved you talked to James Currey. We have worked together for a long time and I feel I can straighten things out with him in a satisfactory way. So your letter is a big help ...

... I have heard already that Mary Benson has arrived in Botswana and will be in Gaborone for three months. She is, I hear, to stay at the guest house where a friend of mine lives and I asked this friend to find out what brings Mary Benson back to Botswana. She is famous for her beautiful biography on *Tshekedi Khama*.

The politics of Botswana is very cautious and maybe in a sense, Seretse Khama gets credit for this. He is as bewildering to the people of this country, as he is to all the Boers and Rhodesians. His behaviour here is that of royalty dedicated to stuffing its own pocket. He has amassed a lot of private wealth and all his family display a tremendous selfishness. However, just when people damn the man, he turns around and astonishes them. People say: "Wait, we are still studying this man. We don't understand him." I mean, the government always produces huge moral show-downs with bad whites and bad blacks that have everyone nodding their heads in approval. The greatest shocks people get here are moral ones. There is something right and there is something wrong, so people vote for the same government, partly because there is no equal and partly because the present show is stable and everyday. Your vision will come later and with another man in power, more able to deal with the southern African situation than Seretse; more friendly and trusting. I have seen some astonishingly truthful people in this country. Indeed, half the reason I write so well about the country is because of all people told me about themselves. Out of this good climate they could produce a number of good leaders. It is the present I do not trust with rosy glasses; there's lots of complicated undertones. Do you think a leadership of unbridled capitalistic interest is more of a salvation to the country than a Marxist approach? This is the impression conveyed; that the banks will not be nationalised, that nothing will injure investment, such as happened in Zambia and Tanzania; and so everyone heaves a sigh of relief. I am certain of nothing. But all you do say is possible. I don't know about Namibia at all, but African liberation will proceed, that's for sure.

Enclosed is a picture of Howard and me.

As ever,
Bessie

[95]

Dear Randolph,

This is a special letter, just written because it has to be written.

When you wrote that Mary Benson was coming to Botswana, I certainly did not know what to do with the information. Then, the University of Botswana invited me as a guest speaker to a conference on writing over April 2nd-4th. When I left on April 1st, it was announced over the radio that Mary Benson was giving a talk in Gaborone on her relationship with Tshekedi Khama. It was all removed from me and I had no way of establishing contact with her.

When I arrived at Gaborone, Friday 2nd, I was absolutely knocked flat by one of the most astounding events of my life! Mary Benson had heard that the University had invited me. She phoned them in great excitement to arrange a meeting between us. As soon as I put my bags down at the Botswana Training Centre, where I was staying, in she walked, with a glowing face. I have never seen such a beautiful woman in my life before! She informed me that she had read all my books, that I was very well known in England as a writer and that was her excuse for sticking to me like glue the whole day. I met my twin soul. We say identical things.

I told her that you had told me she was in Botswana and she asked many questions about you, seeming not to know you so well. I have never recovered from the meeting. I saw her the whole of Friday 2nd and she gave me a very flashy coat as a gift, costing about R120. It had been given to her as a gift by a rich Johannesburg friend, but it was too small for her. It is all-wool, a bright sun-yellow, with a very stylish cut. Gaborone was pouring with rain all the while I was there, so I flashed around in a million dollar garment I could not afford to buy in a thousand years!

Meeting Mary Benson, is like meeting perfection itself. If you wish to meet her you can certainly use me as an excuse. ... I turned down a lecture tour of England last year because I was to terrified to take it on and I don't see the day when I won't be terrified and insecure! Try writing to the British Embassy here about entry into England as a stateless person and you won't like the sort of letter you receive.

Mary Benson is absolutely friendly and absolutely sound in the head. It is more of a spiritual experience meeting her than anything else. She is having some trouble writing her memoirs, which are very valuable; notebooks on Malawi/Nyasaland; notebooks on her involvement in liberatory movements in South Africa. She seems to lack the drive that created her great book — *Tshekedi Khama*.

Mary Benson is the most lovely person in the world to meet. She is second only to one other person I have met so far in sheer delight to know. She will talk as though she is uncertain and floundering; but I love that. I am too.

As ever, Bessie

[96]

P.O. Box 15, Serowe
9 May 1976

Dear Randolph,

I write this letter because it seems as though my better judgement has finally deserted me and from now on I may err and do the wrong thing all the way. I hope your better judgement may help me.

I have not sorted my affairs out yet and I haven't the nerve or resources left to face what might happen over the next two months.

I am not sure what is happening at the firm of Davis-Poynter Ltd.

(a) They are packing up under the stress of inflation OR

(b) I have not been a money spinner for them so I need not get replies to letters or contracts signed until I break up completely as punishment for not being a money spinner.

I have no way of verifying point (a). Perhaps you know.

Here are the facts for point (b).

For *A Question Of Power*, Davis-Poynter sold 796 copies over three years. It did not cover costs. I was a dead loss there. I have 5,000 fans in England. From statements, those fans bought up both my earlier books in hardcover. With inflation, they were off hardcover. Everyone waited for the paperback and when Heinemann came out, those 5,000 bought the book all right. James Currey, almost immediately on publication, sent Davis-Poynter royalties of £ 43.86 of which £21.93 was to come to me. This was retained by Davis-Poynter as I had not covered costs. Some fans who write to me stated that they could no longer rise to hardcover editions but would wait for paperback. Nothing will change this situation in England …

… I write this letter because I need someone behind me for what is going to happen next. Davis-Poynter isn't going to write. Two more months may go by. Nothing will be done. I have no resources at all to live on and I am at the end of my tether.

I am capable of writing Davis-Poynter a very reasonable letter stating my situation exactly. I am not going to earn any money for a hardcover publisher in England. He said he would contract the short stories for £300. I am at the point where I have lost my better judgement and do not want to contract to him. I want him to release the collection.

I simply need someone in London to receive the collection from Davis-Poynter. Immediately after this, it would not matter that Heinemann want it until I can arrange something whereby I won't be a loss there too. I have both the *Serowe* book and the collection of short stories under consideration with Random House Inc., New York and I have to get a final word from them.

Do not involve anyone in this letter. Do not discuss it with James Currey. The mess will only widen and widen without end. Please hold it down and send me your advice. I have written it to bolster myself up against what is coming next — another six months silence on my affairs from Davis-Poynter.

I do not know what has happened to the *Serowe* book. All work was completed on it in June 1975, but nothing more was done to show that it was in production; no jacket design was sent for approval; nothing.

I know things are pretty bad in England but this situation is murderous. I would rather be free of it.

If it would be an embarrassment for you to receive the collection of short stories from Davis-Poynter, please tell me so. I shall then arrange for someone else in London to receive it from him. I shall do nothing more until I hear from you.

Enclosed is a copy of my last letter to Davis-Poynter.

As ever, Bessie

[97]

Dear Randolph,

Not long after I had posted my last letter to you, I received a letter from Davis-Poynter and also one from James Currey. I had not *expected* to hear from Davis-Poynter for another two months or so; and was beginning to feel quite hysterical.

I replied to these letters. I do not want to cause hostilities if my work can move forward. It appears, from James Currey's letter, that the *Serowe* book is still in manuscript form in the office of Davis-Poynter. Could you CAREFULLY verify this from James Currey?

I might be able to sort things out at last.

As ever,
Bessie

[98]

Dear Randolph,

I'd written a hasty note to you at the post office during the week and have just received your letter of May 15th. I thought I'd wait for a reply to my letter, was fearful of the mix up of crossing and crisscrossing mail, so that was why I sent the small note.

Yes, I received a letter from James Currey (the one of May 4th you quote), and at the same time a letter from Davis-Poynter. I enclose carbons of both my replies to Davis-

Poynter and James Currey. You will note that the letter to Davis-Poynter is quite straightforward. There is no immediate need for you to contact him in London on my behalf, as he wrote. I did not expect him to. This is what makes me uneasy.

As far back as 20th Nov. '75, Pat Cullinan wrote him a letter, which had business proposals, that had been going on for some time. I had my own thing going with Pat Cullinan ...

... So, still hold everything down for the time being. If I get a satisfactory reply from Davis-Poynter which considers all the points I raised there, then I will proceed and arrange a contract with him for the collection of short stories, with his sub-contract to James Currey. I fear the letter will annoy him but those points had to be straightened out ...

... I laughed and laughed at your comments on F. It's all right. I know how to handle a correspondence fairly carefully and indeed your comments are a benefit I'll keep in mind. You throw her into the category of people who have no love to offer or anything indeed. I laughed because I am as complicated, I have found (as F's London life). When people approach me, as she did, they want something ...

... We had that sort of peculiar conversation where someone wants to tell me everything as though I am the key to something they want. I've had this happen a lot of times and it builds up a terrible pressure because the person is going to stay and force it out of me. And then everything is over. That's what I mean about complicated. I've had this happen a lot of times. I don't usually know what people want until it's over. She might have got it already in those long conversations we had. Her notes, and they are coming thick and fast, are abrupt and short.

Thank you for your offer of help with the Davis-Poynter firm. I'm off the man. He gave me a hell of a time, but if I feel that things are working out the right way I'll sign up with him again and let you know.

As ever,
Bessie

[99]

P.O. Box 15, Serowe
31 May 1976

Dear Randolph,

The enclosed carbon of the letter to Davis-Poynter is so important that I am sending this to you by registered post. I do not trust the man and I do not want to contract with him any more. This is a final decision.

I need your help to get it over with. My letter to him may be effective enough to make him hand the typescript over to you and not sue me. It states everything that has to be said. If he won't hand it over, could you just show the carbon of the letter to your lawyer friend and ask what is to be done next. I want that collection free from Davis-Poynter. I could not ask him to hand it over to James Currey in case Davis-Poynter wants to sue me. I have no money. Explain everything to your lawyer friend, if necessary. Please ask him to help me. The terms were as follows. James Currey was to hand over to Davis-Poynter £200 which Davis-Poynter keeps. Then Davis-Poynter sends me £150 as his advance. I stuck it up his arse because after all this time it is useless to me. I am in a desperate position. I told you that I have nothing to live on and Davis-Poynter is playing a deadly game. He's had me on a string for months for £150. I want it up his arse. I have given the horrible bastard a hard boot.

Next, phone James Currey, ONCE you get the collection.

206

Tell him I have to clear myself with Davis-Poynter first, but I am not offering the collection to Davis-Poynter. If James likes, he can do it in paperback right away. You are not free to discuss the letters with him and show him the letter to Davis-Poynter. Tell him to be careful to write direct to me and I shall send him the carbon I have from Davis-Poynter's demise as my so-called publisher. I'll sort out other matters with James Currey like who he sub-contracts to. Tell him this could not be helped as I could not straighten out my affairs with Davis-Poynter. He is playing a game and I can't see his cards. I kicked them on the fucking floor and to hell with it all.

As soon as you receive this letter could you please phone Davis-Poynter at his office ...

I hope I do not put you into any trouble. I want to end this nightmare.

As ever, Bessie

[100]

P.O. Box 15, Serowe
25 June 1976

Dear Randolph,

Thank you for your note of 16th June and also for collecting my typescripts from Davis-Poynter Ltd. At the same time I received your note, I also received a letter from James Currey, so I am enclosing carbons of my letters to you both.

I feel a sense of relief more than anything else as I feel my affairs can at last be sorted out with people who make sense to me.

Could you please do the following with the typescripts:

1. *Botswana Village Tales:*

Please hand this collection of short stories, *Botswana*

Village Tales directly to James Currey. James certainly wants it, so that is all that has to be done. I'll work out further details with James.

2. *Serowe: The Village of the Rain-Wind.*

Randolph, count up my postage bill against the day I unexpectedly become a millionaire. Note it, because I would like you to return the top copy and the revised pages to me. I shall have to make a number of complicated arrangements about this typescript, so I need to have it with me ...

... I am extremely grateful for your help at this time, Randolph. A mess like this would not have occurred had I been dealing with people who are straight-forward. Would you choose the cheapest way to post *Serowe: The Village of the Rain-Wind* back to me. If you could register it I would be grateful.

Thank you very much.

As ever,
Bessie Head

[101]

P.O. Box 15, Serowe
23 July 1976

Dear Randolph,

I received your telegram yesterday. It's quite all right that you have posted back *Botswana Village Tales*. James was going to post it to me anyway.

You will find enclosed a carbon of a letter to James Currey which sets *Botswana Village Tales* in order ...

... I am going to do a long haul on *Serowe*. If an American publisher will take it, well and good. Next, there is a publisher in Norway whose attention was brought to my work.

They want it for aid agency work and have already been in touch with me. All the aid agency people had to use *When Rain Clouds Gather* as an introduction to Botswana. There was nothing else.

I am certainly not a dog or a beggar. My work has earned respect but as I say, I've had a bad run of luck with ill and evil people.

Thank you very much for your help.

As ever,
Bessie

The first half of 1976 brought a rush of letters, almost solely about Bessie's running battles with her publishers and agents. More than half the contents have been omitted because they are wounding and probably libellous, and because, to all but a tiny few interested in the minutiae of author-publisher arrangements, they are tedious to read. What remains gives the flavour of the rest, and includes a few flashes of the old Bessie, both the defiant and the "terrified and insecure"

She developed fierce hatreds of those she did business with, though in time the intensity would abate. Much of this was because of her remoteness and isolation, though some of her bitterest attacks were on people who had come to see her from South Africa.

My own letters say much about Namibia, Botswana's neighbour, where, with the collapse of Portuguese rule in Angola, freedom from South Africa's illegal occupation was at last coming into view. There was little response from Bessie, in her preoccupation with her publishing and tax tangles. Her views in her letter of 18 February 1976 were prompted by my writing:

> I try to tell myself that Namibia is not heading for statehood dominated by three of my chief horrors: totalitarianism, tribalism and Marxism-Leninism. I have many friends in Swapo as opposed to the trio as I am and hope they can stay at or near the top. [We must] work towards some sort of democracy that allows human rights yet combats economic exploitation.

Botswana Village Tales came out as *The Collector of Treasures* in 1977, from Heinemann Educational Books, who have remained Bessie's British publisher. I had met the literary agent John Johnson with one of his authors, C.J.Driver, ten years earlier and liked him, as did Jonty Driver, who found him also helpful and effective. Bessie was taken on by his agency and the relationship survived.

6. Iowa-Berlin-Serowe

14 September 1977 -11 July 1979

[102]

1110 North Dubuque St, Iowa City, Iowa 52240, U.S.A.

14 September 1977

Hiya Randolph,

It's been ages since I last heard from you and you owe me a letter. I left Botswana in frantic haste for America and here I am half way round the world.

The American Embassy in Gaborone nominated my name to attend an international writing programme at the University of Iowa as from this month until the 31st Dec. We have then ten days of travel in America but I may opt out of that and go home.

I never thought I would get to see the world and I thought I ought to go before I kick the bucket. Howard I hope is safe. I tried to fix everything for him before I left but I have not yet had news from home to say all is well with him. He is being looked after by one of his form teachers.

We are attached for the programme to the University of Iowa but our routine is quiet and protected , with lots of time to get on with our own work. I chose these four months to sort out my writing life which has been in a mess for a long time. James will be bringing out a collection of short stories by about Sept. 18th and I know he will give you a copy any-

211

way since you are friends. Or please ask him if you would like one.

I shot through Heathrow airport on August 16th in one hour and took a Pan-AM flight straight on to New York. Most of the last nine days have been spent rushing around sorting out food and living here. I am on a State Department grant and living it up in a gorgeous apartment with all sorts of gadgets when a month ago I had nothing to my name and was in considerable despair. I cannot help laughing at the twist of fate because just before this I received a terrible letter from a New York publisher, who had agreed to collaborate with Heinemann on the short stories. They wanted to skin me absolutely dry. They actually wrote asking me to sign over the stories to them absolutely for free with no advances and almost non-existent royalties. They ordered 1500 copies from Heinemann. The State Department letter came at the same time, with a living allowance of $1,000 a month. I asked them to cancel the order with Heinemann and am trying to get Doubleday to take it on. I haven't had a reaction from James but I sent him some frantic letters. ... Africana publishing company wrote saying that they offer me nothing because they are a scholarly [*rest of letter missing*]

Bessie

[103]

1110 North Dubuque St., Iowa City, Iowa 52240, U.S.A.
4 October 1977

The correct, neat American way of greeting is: Hi. So here goes —

Hi Randolph,

Enclosed you will find a copy of a letter to James which

explains my writing affairs to date. *The Collector Of Treasures* is only coming out in the U.K. in paperback, but it will be in hardcover with David Philip, Cape Town.

I was only granted a 24 hour visa to transit through London on the 30th August and I doubt I would be able to arrange a stop over of any kind on my way back because I am travelling on a United Nations Refugee travel document. I hadn't any plans like that anyway, so I'll most probably be heading home around the beginning of January.

I am due to give a few talks at the University of Quebec, Canada, but things have not been finalised yet. The man who invited me is Cecil Abrahams, a relative of the writer, Peter Abrahams. He mentioned in his letter that he knew Harold. I informed him that we have no communication. I had asked Harold to divorce me and there are some simple ways of doing this. He did not reply. He is in Toronto ... No one wanted to marry me anyway. I am 40 now. But it would have made life tidy and concluded everything. I hope not to see him.

It's very nice out here. We live in the Bible belt of America and the group of writers I am with have been taken out on fairly long tours to other nearby cities. All along the route, in between huge bill-boards advertising food for road travellers are equally huge bill boards telling people to watch out for their souls: WHAT WOULD IT PROFIT A MAN IF HE GAIN THE WHOLE WORLD AND LOSE HIS OWN SOUL IN THE END.

Astonishingly, in the midst of haste and technology is a community, the Amish people who live stubbornly in the 18th century. They are of German origin and refuse to touch machines and progress, which is "the devil's work." The men and women live isolated from the rest of the community much as the early old pioneers did. I enclose two post cards of the Amish people. You will note that they still

213

plough in the old way. We visited a large agricultural manu-
facturing concern, John Deere, which produced air-condi-
tioned cab tractors for $90,000!

Life is bad here, with big teeth. I saw on television the
other night that the farmers arranged a big protest against rising costs and said they were running at a loss. The farmers
were all in their sweat shirts with placards and they needed
$6.00 a bushel for their wheat to make ends meet. A pretty
man in a tie had the last word. He said the farmers would
wreck America. Canadian wheat was only $3.00 a bushel and
if they gave the farmers $6.00 a bushel everyone would go for
Canadian wheat and America would become a residual sup-
ply. No talk of subsidy for farmers!

Life is very quiet and secluded here. Iowa city is a small
university town and nothing more than that. It has a popula-
tion of 50,000 people. Serowe is 40,000, so I cannot help feeling at home. I live in a big apartment building with 26 other
writers from all around the world and share an apartment
with a girl … She's not so nice. She's a terrible fuck-about.
It's just that that sort of woman does not like other women
because they spend a lot of time taking other women's men
from them. I don't think they value men either. She just
sleeps around because that's her life style of the wealthy so-
called upper class in the Philippines — the sort who spends
$300.00 on perfume. I try to keep out of her way as much as
possible and I can lock my apartment up. We share the bathroom and kitchen. Her lovers are messy and piss on the toilet seat. She's been sleeping around with some of the male
writers — we are in the proportion of 20 males to six
females. She's going to New York for a month because Iowa
City and its dull routine is almost death to her.

We do have a hell of a routine. A large amount of time has
been allocated for our own work. I brought along the novel

on Khama the Great and at the same time I am bashing out a collection of historical short stories. I can work the whole day and the whole evening in an uninterrupted way and there have truly been some days when I have had a nightmare sense of detachment from the world. Four or five solid days can go by like this and I am only too keen to get lost in sustained work but even I surface with horror before the discipline. We only have to meet once every Friday afternoon in a seminar and give a talk against the background of our own countries. Apart from that we are on our own. The apartment is full of gadgets to provide leisure from work and a washing machine and spin dryer at the end of the corridor. So there's not much to do except work. I thank God I have a heavy research routine for the Khama book.

Howard is 15. He's very safe and being cared for by a form teacher. He's writing his Junior Certificate exam. He's in good hands with a very severe discipline. He has to be home at six p.m. each day, have supper and go to his room to study. He writes to me because I send him things every two weeks, some pretty clothes and bubble gum. But mostly he's a devil when I'm around, arguing with me all the time and quarrelling. I must say I like these four months freedom from motherhood, and Botswana.

As ever, Bessie

Citizenship Office, Ministry of Home Affairs, Gaborone
5 October 1977

Dear Madam,

APPLICATION FOR CITIZENSHIP

I regret to inform you that after careful consideration, your application for citizenship was not successful.

Yours faithfully,

T.B.G. Habangaan for / CITIZENSHIP OFFICER

[104]

1110 North Dubuque St., Iowa City, Iowa 52240, U.S.A.

14 December 1977

Dear Randolph,

I haven't yet got my flight bookings confirmed but I pass through London either the 10th or 11th January 1978 on my return to Botswana. The State Dept. people could have got me a visa for a week's stop over in London but I have been so depressed that I declined the offer. I have a commitment to see Rex Collings who has my *Serowe* book and I shall try to see him between the time the plane lands at about 7 a.m. to the time I take a flight for Lusaka at 7 p.m. in the evening. A friend, Jane Grant, may drive me to his office.

Early this year I applied for Botswana citizenship. A letter was forwarded to me here stating that my application had been rejected. I'd tried to get some security for Howard. So, there's not much to go home to. I have been a tremendous asset to Botswana as a lot of people working on international aid programmes used my books for their work in the country.

So I'd rather go straight through and see what I do next. So one is depressed, you see.

Bessie

[105]

P.O. Box 15, Serowe
27 January 1978

Dear Randolph,

This is the first opportunity I have to write since I've come back to thank you for that very lovely day in London. It was such a pleasure to meet you after all these years. You haven't aged much except that your hair is on the thin side. I enjoyed the day tremendously.

After I'd left you all everything went wrong. Our flight broke down. We boarded the plane and at take-off time the engine would not start. So we disembarked and sat in the airport until 2 a.m. Then it was announced that the engine trouble was so bad it would take some time to fix so we were put on a bus and driven an hour away to a Brighton hotel. Then driven back again at 8 a.m. on the 11th Jan. to Gatwick. It was a situation where our whole existence hung on airport announcements. After three sleepless nights I finally landed in Botswana. I found the people at the American Embassy absolutely frantic. They had cabled Washington who could only trace me as far as Heathrow airport. Then I seemed to disappear into thin air. They showed me frantic cables they'd sent in all directions trying to trace me. Air Botswana did not report the breakdown in London. So things have been rather muddled but here I am. Thank you so much for a wonderful day.

As ever,
Bessie

[106]

P.O. Box 15, Serowe
21 May 1978

Dear Randolph,

Thank you for the enclosed short story from the *Guardian*. Anna Cooper represents me at the John Johnson agency and I left with her a batch of historical short stories. I am very uncertain of the historical work I have been doing for some time — a portion of the life of Khama the Great. I had to cover the whole of southern Africa for him to give me a good starting point, so some of my research was superfluous to my novel and these I worked into short stories. They are not flamboyant me taking off in full flight, but restrained, disciplined work. I am so uneasy with the results, fearing that the work is stiff and lifeless. The one great benefit I have is that I have made myself thoroughly familiar with the history of southern Africa but I am truly uneasy with this field of work. I've never plodded like this before and I quake and quake all the time. Anna Cooper told me she sold one of the historical short stories to *London Magazine* called "A Period of Darkness" and that they are to publish it in July. She may try the *Guardian* with some of the others she has.

Anna Cooper also wrote and told me that Heinemann had approached her for a look at the *Serowe* book and that she would be in touch with me shortly about their decision.

I think it is bound to be as bewildering, Southern Africa, as bewildering as its past. I have lived here where the past history was the least complex — it could be said because the land was so harsh and undesirable and where it was too difficult to wrest a living. Some of wealth that doomed South Africa (the diamonds) were only discovered here after independence. I fear that the countries that have suffered after independence and are going to suffer, have been the ones where people lived in fear. I had to live a long time with the police here as I reported at the police camp every Monday for 13 years and seeing the police for so long was as pleasant as my daily round here. I don't think Moçambique and Angola are a bed of roses. I stopped over in Luanda, Angola, briefly as the plane had to re-fuel and our plane was met by the army with guns, really obtrusive and frightening. That's the Portuguese heritage. The Boer heritage is far worse and the news from Namibia is very very ominous indeed. Do you think the Boer will ever let go?

Buthelezi is the Boers' prize show. He turns up everywhere in South Africa and it looks like it is only those sorts of men they are prepared to have dealings with. Some of the men, impatient for power, (and these men were on the outside) have bought their way in, like the Buthelezi way. I know some who have done it in Namibia, hence the assassinations and riots you hear about. I am totally blank about the leadership qualities of Sam Nujoma and I wonder if he is one of the personal friends you mention. A rival once described him in my presence as a fool. I knocked about on the revolutionary fringe, and refugeeism touches that, and it made me shudder.

Robert Sobukwe died. I loved the man deeply and I have since his death been looking over some things he wrote. He worried about the very thing you mention but like a question. A planned economy and democracy have not yet succeeded, he wrote, in any country that has tried the experiment so far. Can we not secure the two in South Africa. Do we not guarantee the highest when we guarantee human rights? I knew he was a rich and creative man, but looking over his papers it never struck me before that he was also so idealistic. The light went out for me with his death. For days and days I cried simply because he was the only man I loved and trusted.

As ever,
Bessie

[107]

Dear Randolph,

I was in Berlin and have just received your letter of the 9th June. I met James Currey and Lewis Nkosi there, so they have all the Berlin news, including its disasters. James wanted me to come on to London but I had not arranged things properly at home and Howard only had care for three weeks. As for my news, you may have heard that I was suddenly offered citizenship in February this year after my application had been rejected two years ago. I accepted the offer because it simplified my life.

The big agricultural man here is Vernon Gibberd. He's British and he's married to a woman from Holland. He worked for a long time here in Serowe Brigades from 1969 to about 1978. Prior to that he worked for many years at Tshekedi Khama's Bamangwato Development Farm, where he did a lot of research into agriculture under drought conditions. He is roughly the "Gilbert" of *When Rain Clouds Gather*. I certainly worked with him for five months at Tshekedi's farm and a lot of the agricultural material in *Rain Clouds*, I took from him. I worked again with him in Serowe when I was building up the communal garden because he used to order our materials and offer advice. I like his agricul-

220

tural papers. He has a very lyrical style and the man is like that, an exceedingly pleasant, harmonious personality. You only meet him at a very superficial level because he likes his inner life to be well-hidden from public view, but the superficial level is exceedingly enjoyable. He talks to people very easily and quickly. He knows everything that's going on and has a vast store of gossip about people ...

... It was a surprise to us when he resigned from Brigades and took up work for the government. He would never have done so had he not wanted to. He has the total view of the aid situation in Botswana and would be the best person to advise your son about possible opening for work. Your son could use my name as an introduction. I always write flaming letters to people and it's usually dead accurate. No one holds it against me because it's the truth. It's simply me and people are used to me just like that. I am sure Vernon Gibberd will respond to his enquiry and would be able to explain the Botswana situation to him.

I have a mess here at home cleaning and tidying up after an absence of three weeks, so this is just a short note.

As ever,
Bessie

6

During her first visit out of Africa — to the United States in 1977 — which I had heard about before she wrote, I urged her to stop over in London. I arranged for a few friends to meet her at the Goring Hotel in Victoria before she caught her flight from Gatwick to Gaborone. We had tea together, with Myrna Blumberg, Ken Mackenzie, James Currey, Betty Sleath and perhaps one or two others. Bessie and I had not seen each other for 13 years. She was older, stouter, and darker from the Botswana sun. She was polite and a little formal, but her voice and precise manner of speech were unchanged. There was too little time and we were too large a group to allow any relaxed talk of the past or present. As if to dampen our prospects of a joyful reunion, we were caught in a downpour on our way to the Goring. I wrote to Bessie, in response to her somewhat stilted letter of thanks:

> It was lovely seeing you, tho' so briefly, and ending with all of us straggling through the grim backways of Victoria Station to see you into that British Caledonian waiting room, like a staging post to the Next World. What an anticlimax to an anticlimax that you had to wait half the night at Gatwick, thence to Brighton ...

The last few letters were replies to mine at intervals of many months. When I wrote in June 1979 I mentioned that my son, just down from the university, was looking at agricultural development in Africa, and asked "Do you think there are openings in Botswana?" Her suggestion that he use her name in approaching Vernon Gibberd called forth the recollection of another clash, best left unquoted here. Still, she felt, her "flaming letters" did not sever relationships permanently. This misconception of the effect of her broadsides and the infallibility of her judgements did poor Bessie much harm over the years.

* * *

And with that her letters to me ended — those that have survived. She kept a few of my letters and Christmas cards into the 1980s. In June 1983, replying to a lost letter of hers, I commiserated over some unstated problem and ended: "Is there a book due? James hasn't mentioned one. I do hope so, or that you are finding yourself able to write as you want at present", suggesting another difficulty of the time. But my object had been to introduce a nephew, Stephen Thompson, going out, between school and university, to teach near Gaborone, and to ask if he could visit her. Her letter after the event is missing too. He arrived, I learned later, with two friends, all of whom slept at Rain Clouds, but she made no complaint and wrote glowingly about him.

Our last meeting was in 1980, when James Currey asked me to meet Bessie and Howard at Heathrow and drive them to Heinemann's in Bedford Square. They were to stay a few nights with Jane and Neville Grant, Jane having become a regular correspondent of Bessie's while researching an M Phil on African writing. At our flat in Kensington Bessie talked about the brouhaha she had created en route, when, in Copenhagen, she and Ngugi wa Thiong'o, once a *New African* contributor and now a successful novelist, had said hard things about Karen Blixen's racial attitudes in a television interview. The press had carried it on and Bessie clearly enjoyed being the storm centre, categorising her attack with the "flaming letters" and her pronouncements as "dead accurate." The Danes, it seemed, were not used to her and did not accept the truth of her charges against the Baroness, a revered writer and their cherished literary link with Africa. Denmark's generosity in setting up and maintaining the Khama III Memorial Museum, with its Bessie Head archive, in Serowe is the more to be commended.

My last recollection was of her sitting, smoking and talking in our drawing room, an old friend with whom it would take longer than we had to make up for the flown years. James Currey was with us and I told Bessie how I owed my liberty to James, who had smuggled me out of South Africa in 1964, at great risk to himself, when she was already teaching in Botswana. James had worked with *The New African* both in Cape Town and London, where Lewis Nkosi, Bessie's most perceptive critic, had been literary editor.

Her stay was taken up with Heinemann business and we did not go to the party they had for her, hoping for another time to meet and talk as friends. But all that followed were my few letters, reduced in number by an overwhelming business dispute in 1980-2, involving protracted litigation, which is second only to hanging for concentrating a man's mind. I wrote on a card for Christmas 1982: "I follow your books with pleasure and admiration ... Do let me know if you are to be in England". *Serowe: Village of the Rain Wind* came out in 1981, but though Bessie had sent me an early draft of the introductory material about Tshekedi, I can find no comments on it. I felt she was in the hands of agents and publishers and, overstretched myself, did not respond to her doubts about her capacity to write history. A time would come.

I felt no longer part of her private life. It had been, she wrote in *Serowe: Village of the Rain Wind*, made up of "shattered little bits" and in Botswana they had begun to grow together into a whole. Botswana was a case of initial loathing turning in time to love, the reverse of the process with so many she had known. There would still be a chance, in time, to visit her in Botswana.

The news of her death in April 1986 meant that our friendship could not be revived, nor, infinitely sadder, her greatest books written. I cabled Pat van Rensburg in Gaborone:

PLEASE CONVEY TO HOWARD FOR BESSIE HEAD FUNERAL: WE MOURN A DEAR AND VALUED FRIEND AND A RARE TALENT THE WORLD HAS LOST. DEEPEST SYMPATHY RANDOLPH VIGNE AND FAMILY

Index